CW01123874

Why can't computer books be easier to understand?

Not all of us want to become computer professionals, but we do want to have fun with our computers and be productive. The new *Simple Guides* cover the popular topics in computing. Most importantly, they are simple to understand. Each book in the series introduces the main features of a topic and shows you how to get the most from your PC.

Simple Guides – No gimmicks, no jargon, no fuss

Available in the *Simple Guides* series:

The Internet	Web design
Searching the Internet	Using spreadsheets
The PC	Using email
Office 2000	Putting audio and video on your website
Windows 98	Writing for your website
E-commerce	Dreamweaver 4
Digital cameras, scanning and using images	
Internet research	

A simple guide to
Flash 5 for Windows

**Brian Salter &
Naomi Langford-Wood**

Prentice Hall

An imprint of PEARSON EDUCATION

Pearson Education Limited

Head Office:
Edinburgh Gate
Harlow
Essex CM20 2JE
Tel: +44 (0)1279 623623
Fax: +44 (0)1279 431059

London Office:
128 Long Acre
London WC2E 9AN
Tel: +44 (0)20 7447 2000
Fax: +44 (0)20 7240 5771
website: www.informit.uk.com

First published in Great Britain in 2001
© Brian Salter and Naomi Langford-Wood 2001

ISBN 0-130-61031-3

The rights of Brian Salter and Naomi Langford-Wood to be identified as the authors of this work have been asserted by them in accordance with the Copyright, Designs and Patents Act 1988.

British Library Cataloguing-in-Publication Data
A catalogue record for this book can be obtained from the British Library.

All rights reserved. No part of this publication may be reproduced, stored in a retrieval system, or transmitted, in any form, or by any means, electronic, mechanical, photocopying, recording or otherwise, without prior written permission from the publisher.

Many of the designations used by manufacturers and sellers to distinguish their products are claimed as trademarks. Pearson Education Limited has made every attempt to supply trademark information about manufacturers and their products mentioned in this book. All websites reproduced herein are copyright of their owners.

10 9 8 7 6 5 4 3 2 1

Typeset by Pantek Arts Ltd, Maidstone, Kent.
Printed and bound in Italy.

The publishers' policy is to use paper manufactured from sustainable forests.

Contents

Introduction xiii
How do I use this book? xiii
Adopted conventions xiv
About the authors xv

1 The basics 1

System requirements 2
Software installation 2
Vectors vs bitmaps 9
Streaming delivery 9
Getting to know the Flash environment 10
    The Timeline 10
    The Stage 12
    The Toolbox 15
    Rulers and grids 15
    Testing your Flash 5 movies 18

2 Drawing and painting ...19

Creating basic shapes and objects ...20
    Line tool ...20
    Oval tool ...21
    Rectangle tool ...24
    The pencil ...26
    Painting with the Paint Bucket ...29
    Painting with the Brush tool ...32
    The Eraser ...34
    The Ink Bottle ...35

3 Objects ...37

Selecting objects ...38
    Selecting with the Arrow tool ...39
    Selecting with the Lasso tool ...41
    Selecting portions ...42
    Deselecting parts of a selection ...42
Repositioning ...43
Simple editing commands ...45
    Changing line segments ...46
    Reshaping filled areas ...48

Resizing objects 48
    Changing an object's orientation 51
    Alignment 53
Grouping objects 54

4 Type 55

Inserting text 56
Setting type attributes 57
Transforming type 60
Converting type 61

5 Imported artwork 63

Using imported graphics in Flash 64
Acceptable file formats 64
    Importing raster graphics 65
    Importing vector-based graphics 66
    Importing via the Clipboard 67
Converting bitmaps to vector elements 68
Painting with a bitmapped image 71
Using the Magic Wand 76

6 Layers 79

Creating and deleting layers 82
Using the Layers dialog box 84
    Visibility 84
    Locking 84
    Outline colours 84
    Changing a layer's height 86
    Changing the type of layer 86
Using the Timeline to control layers 87
Stacking objects on different layers 89
Guide layers 91
Mask layers 91
Paste in place 95

7 Symbols and instances 97

Accessing libraries, symbols and instances 98
    The Libraries directory 101
    The Library window 102
Creating symbols from graphic objects 105
Creating symbols without conversion 106

Symbols vs objects 107
Changing an instance ... in an instant 108
Swapping one instance for another 112
Breaking the link between instance and symbol 114

8 Animation 115

Animation basics 116
Frame types 116
Making a simple animation 122
    Smoothing your animation 123
Editing multiple frames 125
Setting the frame rate 125
Tweening animation 128
    Motion tweening 128
    Tweening colour changes and fading in and out 131
    Tweening objects that change size 133
    Rotating objects 134
Moving objects along a predefined path 134
Shape tweening 137
    Shape tweening multiple objects 139
    Using Shape Hints to improve your morphing 141
    Getting shape tweens to move along a path 143

Reversing frames 143
Animated masks 144
Saving your animations 145
A note about scenes 147

9 Interactivity 149

Action types 150
    Frame actions 151
Frame labels and comments 154
Some basic actions 156
Buttons 160
    Creating a button 160
Interactivity with buttons 164
On (MouseEvent)s 165

10 Sound 169

How Flash handles sounds 170
Importing sounds 170
Adding sounds to frames 173
Adding sounds to buttons 174
Sync settings 175

      Adding two sounds simultaneously 176

      Start sounds 177

Streaming sounds 178

Making simple edits to your sound files 180

11 Complex interactivity 183

ActionScript 184

Expressions and variables 185

Other actions 192

      Loading new files into your movie 192

      Get URL 193

      Load movie 195

      Tell Target 195

Conditions 201

      If frame is loaded 201

      Looping an animation 203

      If ... Else 204

Incorporating JavaScript 205

Debugging and commenting out your movie 206

Normal and Expert modes 206

Movie Explorer 209

Coloured prompts 211

12 Publishing your movies 215

Optimising your playback 216
Publishing your movies for use on the web 219
Publishing your movies as standalone Flash Player files 221
HTML publishing 223
Displaying alternative images 226
    GIF images 227
JPEG, PNG and QuickTime files 229
Projectors 229
Other image formats 230
Printing 231
    Printing from a Flash movie 231
Conclusion 235

Index 236

Introduction

Since the emergence of the world wide web less than a decade ago, graphic artists have demanded more and more from their software while also requiring fast download times for their finished masterpieces. In the past few years Macromedia's Flash has become the *de facto* standard web design tool for creating interactive animated presentations on the Internet.

Flash is now in its fifth incarnation and works by placing sequences of images along a Timeline, much the same way as traditional cartoon artists produced acetate movies. Flash takes much of the effort out of the creation process by automating many of the tasks that traditional artists have had to do by hand. And it gives you total control over how the elements of the program interact with one another and with the end user.

Deceptively complex pages and animations can be put together in incredibly small files, which download very much faster than traditionally coded HTML pages. Both Netscape Navigator and Microsoft Explorer support the display of Flash files. In short, no serious web developer can afford to be without it.

How do I use this book?

Whenever you get hold of a new program, there's always the temptation to run before you can walk. You bought Flash, after all, to get animated and interactive movies published for use on the web or as standalone files. It can seem a bit tame, therefore, to have to get down to the nitty gritty of learning how to construct simple graphics before you can make them fly. But Flash is not one of those programs that you can busk your way through – at least not if you want to release the tremendous power of the software provided.

So, starting with the basics, this book takes you through the setting up of a Flash movie and explains all you need to know about the Flash environment. Very soon we're off using the drawing and painting tools and learning how to handle objects, insert text and import artwork from other programs.

The fun stuff then comes with the discovery of layers and the use of symbols and putting them to work in creating first basic and then more complex animation, coupled with interactivity and sound.

Finally, it's important to know how Flash can deliver your movies to an audience – via the web, as standalone projectors or even as alternative file formats such as animated GIFs and QuickTime or AVI movie files.

The book contains copious screen shots to help you grasp what is a complex program, quickly and easily.

Adopted conventions

Throughout the book we have included notes, each of which is associated with an icon:

Provides additional information about the subject concerned.

Indicates a variety of shortcuts: keyboard shortcuts, 'Wizard' options, techniques reserved for experts, etc.

Warns you of the risks associated with a particular action and, where necessary, shows you how to avoid any pitfalls.

About the authors

Brian Salter and Naomi Langford-Wood are 21st-century business experts and practical visionaries. Having come from very different backgrounds, they are specialists in all aspects of communication and business usage of Internet technologies and eBusiness and the building of powerful online communities. And they are leading international speakers in this arena.

Because of these core skills, they have increasingly found their company in demand for advice on the use of emerging technologies within business and – in the process – recognised that the cornerstone requirement for all of this commenced with conducting client Internet and communications audits, as a prerequisite to creating effective market positioning and customer-focused Internet strategies for these clients. This approach has led to commissions from companies worldwide – both 'blue chip' and SMEs – to undertake Internet audits and consultations for them.

Together, Brian and Naomi help companies realise their potential by incorporating the new technologies into their business processes as painlessly and profitably as possible while looking after each company's core assets – its people. Founders of The Association of E-Business Professionals (*www.e-biz-pro.org*), they are also fellows of the RSA and IoD.

The basics 1

System requirements
Software installation
Vectors vs bitmaps
Streaming delivery
Getting to know the Flash environment

System requirements

Flash is a powerful authoring environment for creating animated vector graphics, and as such requires a minimum hardware configuration of:

- a Pentium 133MHz processor running Windows 95, 98, 2000 or NT v4 or 5;
- 32MB of RAM;
- 40MB of available disk space.

Although Flash will work with such a configuration, the faster the processor and the larger the amount of available memory, the quicker and easier the software will be to work with.

Flash 5 movies can be played back on a lower-spec machine, however, allowing a wider audience to view your creations using a web browser such as Netscape 3 or later, or Microsoft's IE3.02 or later, using an additional plug-in as required.

Software installation

To install Flash 5, insert the CD-ROM into your drive and the *autorun* feature should start off the InstallShield Wizard which starts the installation process automatically.

You are given the option of installing the 'authoring extensions' of Generator 2, an application that can combine text, graphics and animation 'on the fly'. For the moment, let's load only Flash 5 as we'll have enough to be getting our teeth into for the time being!

*If **autorun** isn't set up to work on your computer for any reason, simply use Windows Explorer to find the **Setup.exe** file on the CD-ROM and double-click on it, which will start installation.*

1: The basics 3

Figure 1.1 The opening screen of Flash 5's installation

In common with most Windows software, you are recommended to close down any other programs that are running, and are then given a screen full of text that spells out the licence agreement.

Next, the installation software suggests that it loads the main program into your *Program Files* directory, but you can choose a new destination folder if you want to by clicking on the **Browse** button and selecting a new directory path (Figure 1.2).

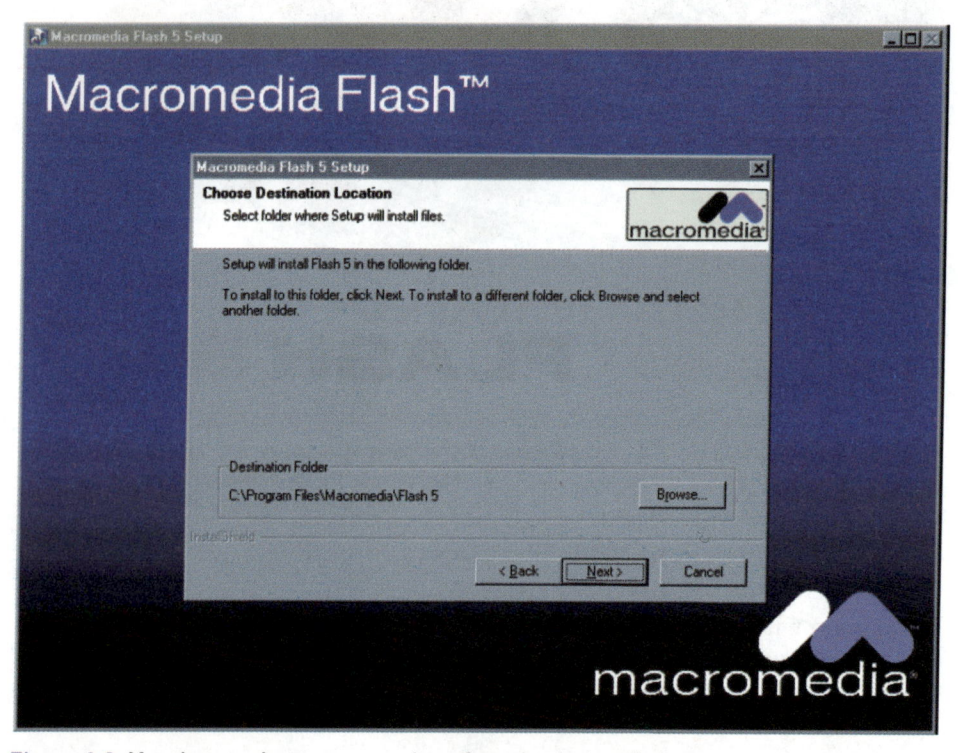

Figure 1.2 You choose where you want the software to be installed

You are now given a choice as to the type of Setup you prefer. You can choose:

- typical – which most people choose. This basically installs the most commonly used options;
- compact – a minimum installation which is useful for those with little spare room on their hard disks;
- custom – where you can choose to install the library of useful, but not essential, files; a selection of sample files; and the get-to-know-you lessons for beginners (Figure 1.3).

Having chosen what you want to install, and where you want to install Flash's files, Macromedia suggests that you install the shortcut files for the program into a start-up directory called *Macromedia Flash 5*. If you're happy with that, click **OK**, or else enter a new name for the directory.

You are also given the option of installing the Flash 5 player plug-in for your browser. Do so, as it would be invidious not to!

You have now given all the information that the program needs to copy across the relevant files, and after a final confirmation screen pops up to ask if you're really, absolutely, 100% sure of your choices (Figure 1.4), installation begins.

Installation is pretty fast, even on the most basic hardware set-up. When the relevant files have been copied across, you should have a *Start:Programs* menu which has all the relevant shortcuts pertinent to your earlier selections, as well as shortcuts to sample pages and Flash players (Figure 1.5).

The only thing left to do is to enter your registration details, which Flash prompts you to do before you are allowed to go any further (Figure 1.6). The

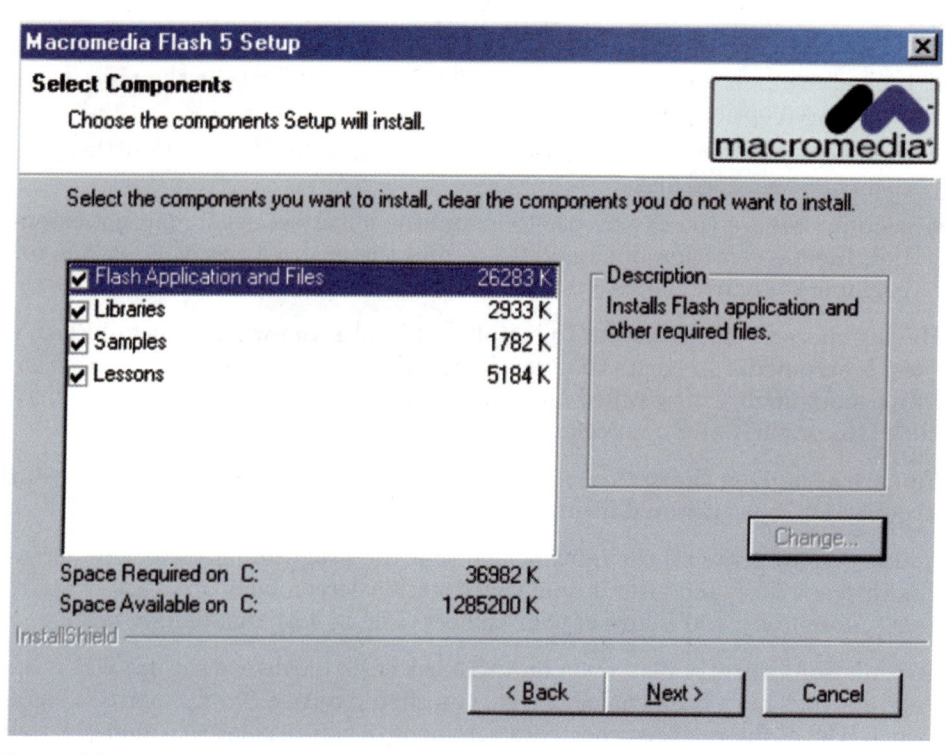

Figure 1.3 A choice of installation is offered

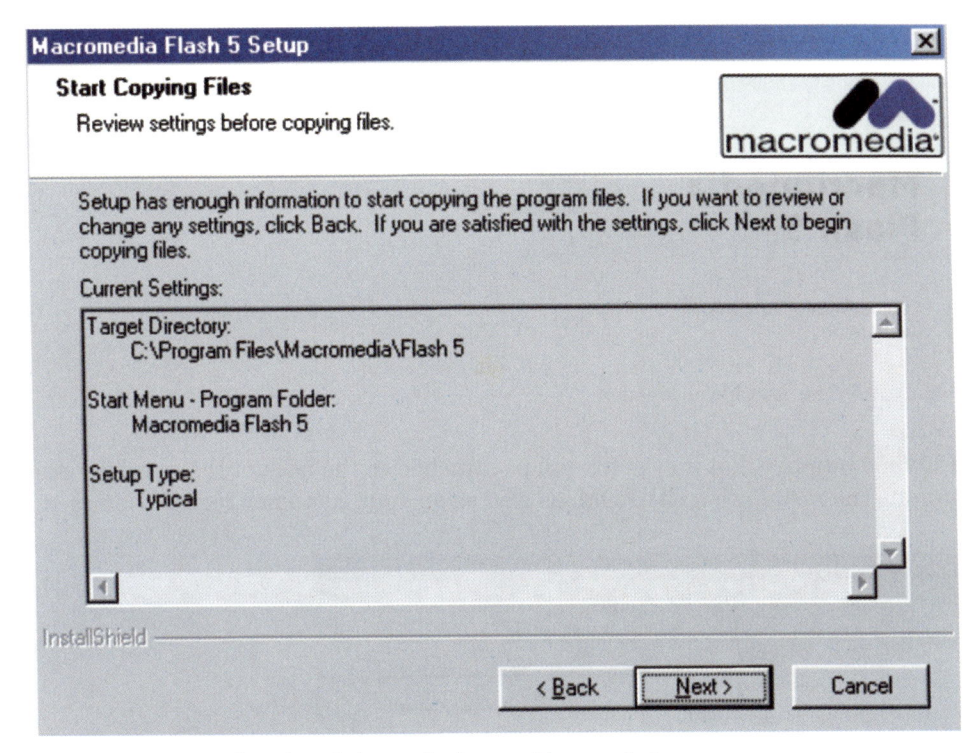

Figure 1.4 Just checking (again) that you're happy with your choices

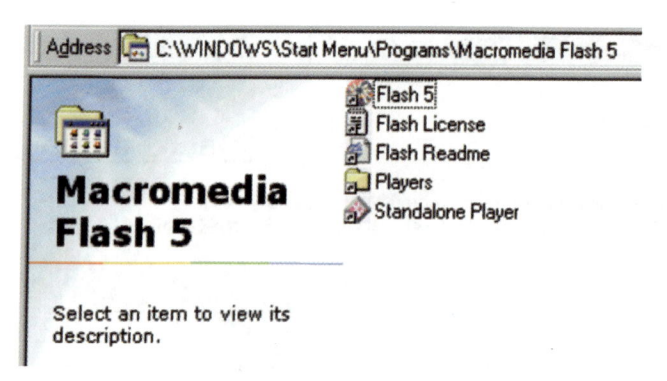

Figure 1.5 The Start Menu selection

FLW500 number that it asks for will be attached to the back of the envelope containing the installation CD-ROM, as well as on your customer registration card.

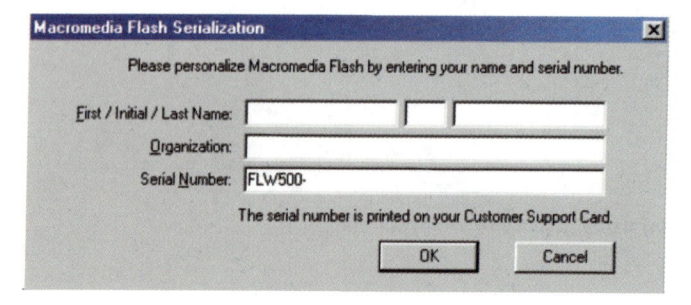

Figure 1.6 You have to enter the serial number of the software before being allowed any further

Vectors vs bitmaps

One of the great strengths of using Flash is that it can handle vector graphics as well as bitmapped files. It is important to understand the difference between the two for a full appreciation of the power that the software gives you.

Traditional image processing programs use bitmap graphics (also known as raster graphics). Here, each individual pixel of an image is defined and the computer is given instructions for every one of them.

The problem comes when you try to resize the graphic. Because pixels are a predetermined size which fit into a grid across your computer screen, resizing can give your image a ragged appearance.

Vector graphics, on the other hand, describe images as a series of mathematical formulae. These include lines and curves, as well as colours and position points. If you resize a vector graphic, its mathematical definition is altered so that the lengths of lines or the position of certain points change, but the overall quality of the graphic is unchanged.

Some file formats such as .gif and .tif files can compress these instructions where there are collections of like pixels. In effect they say to the computer something like: **treat the next 51 pixels identically to this one** *– or whatever.*

Streaming delivery

Another of the strengths of the Flash platform is its ability to stream video or audio. With traditional forms of delivering such files, the user must wait while the whole file downloads before he can watch or listen to the file in question. Obviously, this can mean having to wait some time for the download, especially if it is a big file.

With streaming, on the other hand, playback starts once a portion of the file has downloaded. While you watch the first portion of video, for instance, the second portion downloads, and Flash feeds the frames at a specified frame rate so that the movie appears to be uninterrupted.

Getting to know the Flash environment

When you start up Flash in order to create and edit movies, you will work with the Editor, which consists of a number of areas with which you need to become familiar. The very first time that you start up the software, it loads one of its tutorial files allowing you to familiarise yourself with some of the basics of the Flash 5 working area (Figure 1.7).

- In the top of the window is the area known as the **Timeline**. It is here that you will store the movie's frames, layers and scenes.
- Below this is the **Stage** in which you can see all the graphics that go into making up your movie.
- Situated on the left of the screen is the **Toolbox** which you use to select the various tools you need to edit and create your various movie items.
- The grey area surrounding the Stage is a **work area** in which you can construct various graphic elements, but which does not show in the final movie.

The Timeline

You can think of a Flash movie in the same way as you would a film made for the 'big screen'. A film is made up of a series of scenes. Each scene is made up of a sequence of frames and, just as in a real film, the individual frames play sequentially to give an impression of movement.

The Timeline is where you keep the record of the components of your movie. In it, you store information about the individual frames, and assemble all the artwork into separate layers.

1: The basics

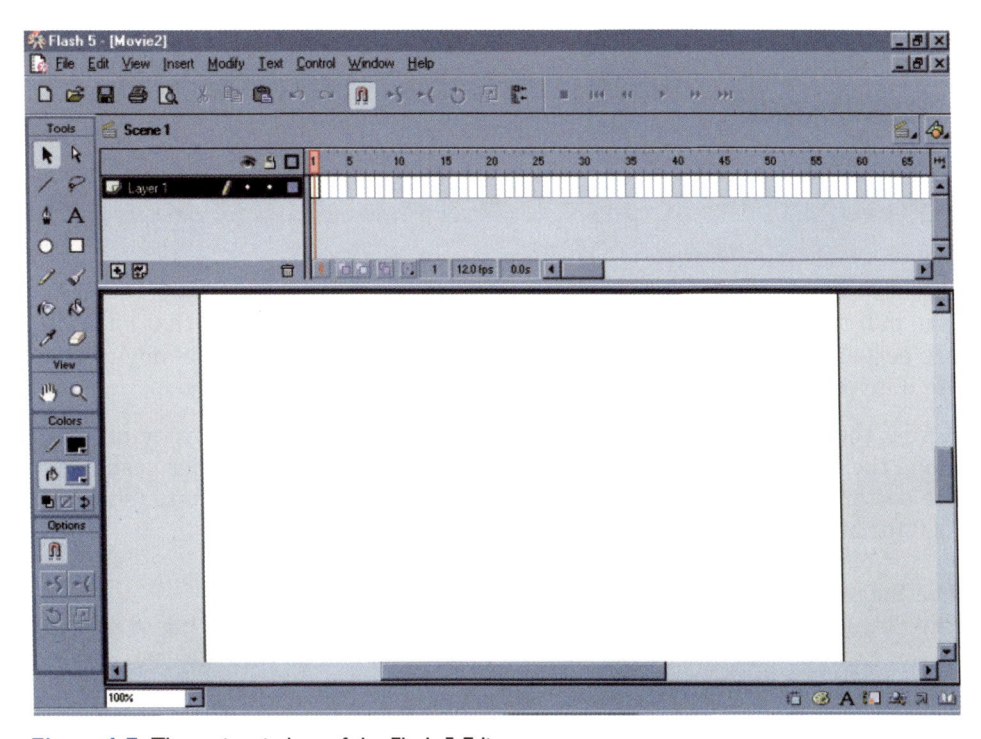

Figure 1.7 The main window of the Flash 5 Editor

If you don't see all the toolbars as shown in Figure 1.7, go to your Window menu and select Toolbars to determine which you want to see and which you want to hide.

Sometimes you will want to hide the Timeline temporarily in order to view the maximum area of stage. You can do this by choosing **Timeline** from the **View** menu or by keying **<Ctrl><Alt>T.**

If you click inside the grey box at the top left of the Timeline (to the left of the eye in Figure 1.8), you can drag the whole of the Timeline into a new position on your screen, either to dock at one of the sides or to float as a separate window on top of anything else on view. If you dock the Timeline horizontally (ie at the top or bottom of the screen), you will increase the number of easily accessible frames. If you dock it to the left or right of the screen, you will see the maximum number of layers.

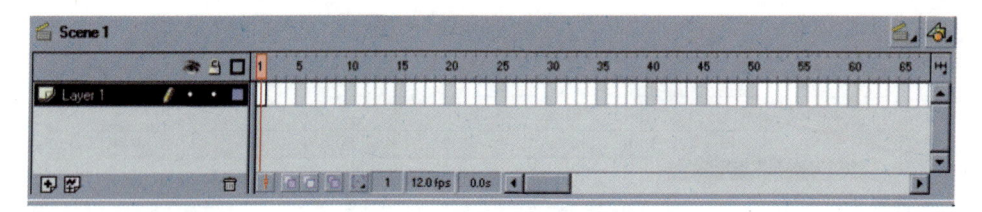

Figure 1.8 The basic Timeline

The individual layers are used to keep your artwork separate so that once they are perfected individually you can combine them into a complete movie scene. We'll investigate layers in Chapter 6.

Across the Timeline the frames are displayed with a 'ruler' of frame numbers along the top of the frames. In addition, the current frame number is shown at the bottom of the Timeline in the box to the left of the Frame Rate (shown as 12.0 fps in Figure 1.8).

The Stage

The Stage is the area in which you will 'stage' your movie. It is as big or as small as you care to make it, but the size you determine will be the size seen by your audience, and will affect the relative positions of all your movie components.

You can control both the size and appearance of the Stage by double-clicking on the frame rate box in the status bar of the Timeline (Figure 1.9).

You will see from Figure 1.9 that you have a number of options for the control of your Stage.

1: The basics

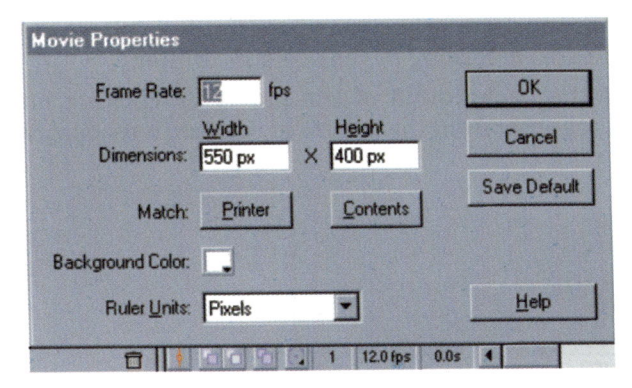

Figure 1.9 The Movie Properties dialog box is accessed by double-clicking the frame rate box

1. The *Frame Rate* controls at how many frames per second the movie runs. For movies viewed over the web, 12 is a good default. Standard films normally run at 25 fps.
2. The *Dimensions* of width and height are where you specify the overall size of the movie. You can specify the dimensions in inches, centimetres, pixels or points. Most people now view the web in a screen resolution of 800 × 600 pixels, although some still view it in 640 × 480 pixels, so it is best to set your dimensions smaller than this.
3. The *Ruler Units* allows you to set the unit of measurements as your default. In Figure 1.9 these are set to Pixels.
4. You can set the size of your Stage to suit the contents of the movie you are working on. Set *Match* by clicking on the **Contents** button, and the Stage

Flash 5 for Windows

will be sized automatically for you. Similarly, clicking on **Printer** will set the Stage to match the printable area according to your default printer.

5. You can set the colour of the background of the movie by clicking on *Background color* and then selecting from the palette of colours that appears (Figure 1.10).

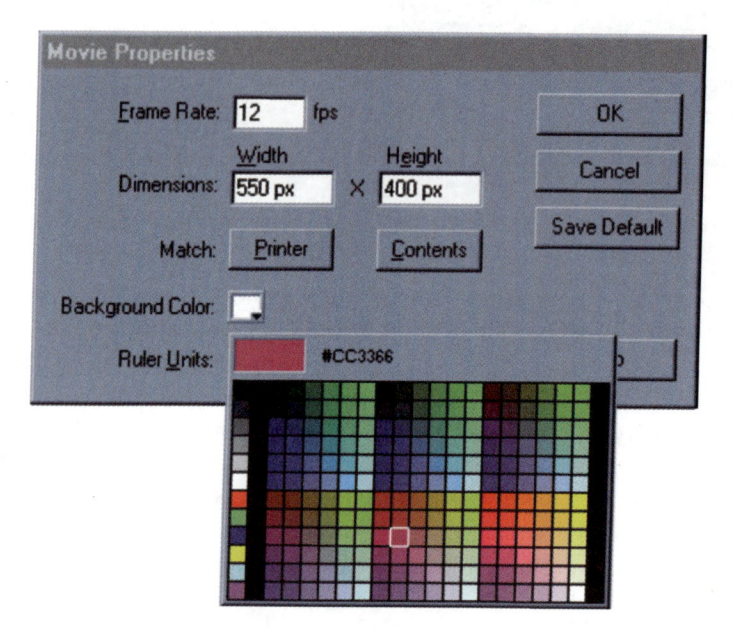

Figure 1.10 Set the Background Color from this colour dialog box

The Toolbox

In the Toolbox are all the tools you will need to draw, select, paint and modify your artwork and objects for animation. Although the Toolbox starts life to the left of your screen, you can also dock it on the right of the screen. Notice that, depending upon which of the tools in the toolbox you have chosen, a set of modifiers is displayed at the bottom of the toolbox. Similarly, the icon bar can be docked at any of the four sides of the screen (shown to the right in Figure 1.11).

Go to the Window menu and you can peruse the selection of **panels** which allow you to view and organise elements within your movie. We'll be using a selection of panels throughout this book.

To help you along the way, Flash gives you the option (turned **on** by default) to show 'tooltips' whenever you hover your mouse over an icon (Figure 1.12). You can set your preferred default by going to the **Edit** menu and selecting **Preferences**.

Rulers and Grids

Together with rulers, you can also display a grid, both of which are ideal aids to drawing objects with exact sizes, shapes or positions. You can turn them on by selecting **Rulers** or **Grid** from the **View** menu (Figure 1.13).

You will see that the menu also allows you to snap items to the grid (Figure 1.14). This snap feature can be set to your preferences by accessing the **Edit Grid** menu, which also allows you to specify the colour of the grid and its overall size.

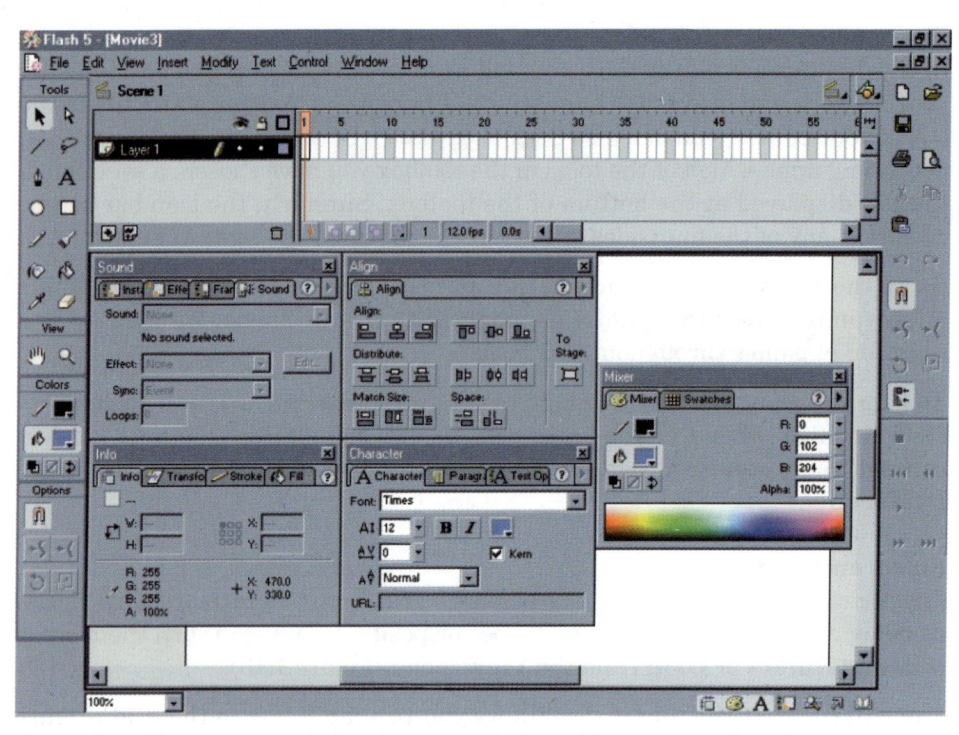

Figure 1.11 The icon bar docked to the right, complete with a selection of panels

1: The basics

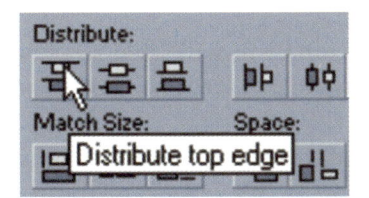

Figure 1.12 Tooltips help you select the right icon

Figure 1.13 Turn on Rulers, Grid and other items from the View menu

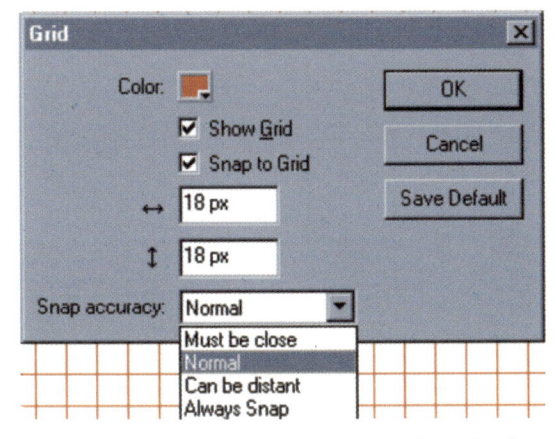

Figure 1.14 Setting your Snap accuracy from the drop-down menu

Testing your Flash 5 movies
As you work through creating your Flash animations you will need to play them back to check that your animations and interactive controls are working properly. There are four basic options:

1. Simple animations and interactive controls can be checked using the Controller toolbar which you turn on by going to **Window:Toolbars: Controller**.
2. You can access the **Test** functions from the **Control** menu.
3. You can test all your animations and controls by creating Flash Player movies that play within a separate window.
4. You can also publish your movie to a web browser.

All the above are covered in detail in Chapter 12, although we will be using the checking features as we work through this book.

Drawing and painting 2

Creating basic shapes and objects

Creating basic shapes and objects

Although Flash lets you import drawings and shapes from other graphics programs, it also allows you to create your own drawings.

On the toolbox you will see a number of icons offering you access to tools such as line drawing, rectangles, ovals and so on. These allow you to create both strokes and fills for a wide variety of basic shapes.

Line tool

Let's start with the **Line** tool. Using this, you can make simple shapes by combining a sequence of lines into, say, a star, a triangle, a pentagon, or whatever.

You can select the Line tool from the Toolbox, or by pressing **N**. Automatically the line modifiers appear at the end of the Toolbox, allowing you to change its colour by clicking on the **Line Color** box (shown as a black square in Figure 2.1). There is also a default black-and-white button which defaults your colour selection to two-colour mode; beside it is another icon (shown as a two-pronged arrow in Figure 2.1) which reverses the colour selection you have made between the stroke and fill colours (we'll come to fills in a moment).

You will undoubtedly want to alter the width of the line as well as what type it is (solid, dashed, dotted, etc) and you can do this in the modifier panels which you open by going to the **Window** and selecting **Panels:Stroke**.

As you click and drag out a line, you will see a hairline representation of the line you are drawing which turns into a line with all the attributes you have assigned only once you let go of the mouse button (Figure 2.2).

Strokes and fills are two terms that appear to have been imported from graphics programs running on Mac machines. Basically, a stroke is an outline, while a fill is a solid. By definition, since lines have no 'insides', they consist purely of strokes. But rectangles, circles and other shapes can have either or both an outline (stroke) and a fill.

2: Drawing and painting 21

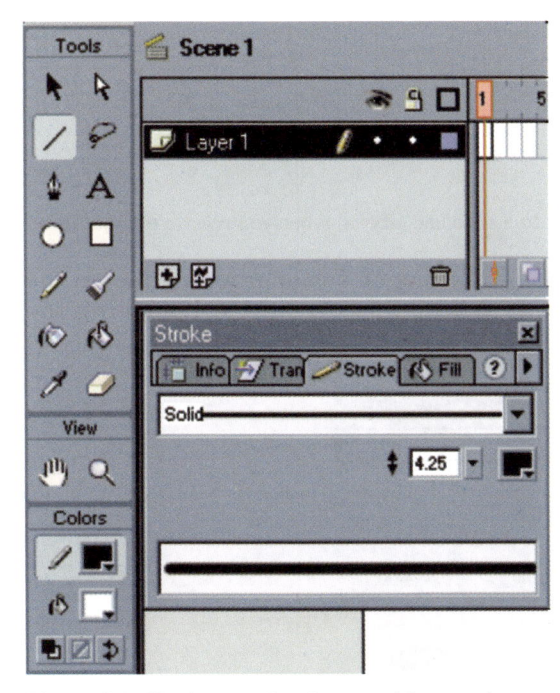

Figure 2.1 The Line tool with its modifier panel

Oval tool
As you would expect, the **Oval** tool allows you to draw ellipses and circles. You can draw them purely as outlines (strokes), as fills (solid colour), or as a combination of the two. You can even fill them with gradients.

If you want to constrain your line to a vertical, horizontal or 45-degree angle, hold down the <Shift> key as you drag your line.

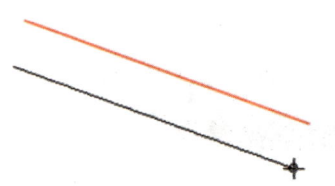

Figure 2.2 The lower line preview turns into a solid line (above) when you release the mouse

You start the Oval drawing process by clicking on the appropriate tool in the Toolbox, or by keying **O**. If you want to draw a perfect circle, hold down the **<Shift>** key as you drag your outline.

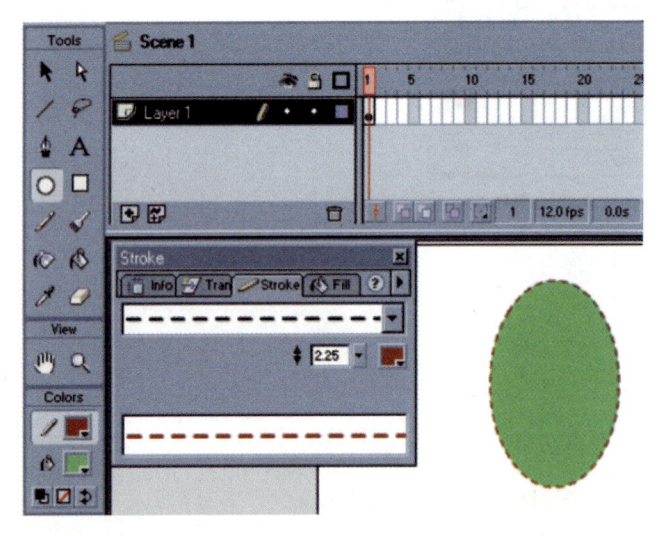

Figure 2.3 The Oval tool, with its modifier panel similar to the Line tool

This time, as well as setting the stroke colour, you can set the colour for the fill. If you look at the panel modifier, you will see you can set the stroke and fill colours from here as well (Figure 2.3).

You have the option of setting either the fill or the stroke to a 'null' colour if you want to have purely a stroke or fill colour respectively. Simply click on the little icon with a red diagonal line in the colour palette (Figure 2.4).

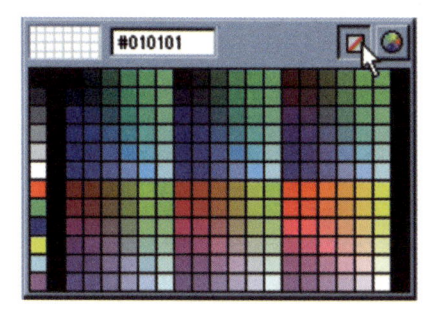

Figure 2.4 Assigning a null colour from the colour chart

If instead of a null colour you wish to assign an actual colour, you can simply check one of the colour boxes in the colour palette. Flash encourages you to use one of the 216 'web-safe' colours – colours that can be resolved by every web browser. However, there is nothing to stop you setting your own colours if you want to. In the **Window:Panels** menu, select either **Mixer** or **Swatches** (Figure 2.5). You can define your own colour swatch, add to or replace colours in the swatch, or revert to the web-safe palette at any time.

Instead of filling an area with solid colour, you can fill with a colour gradient. We'll be covering this in more detail later in this chapter.

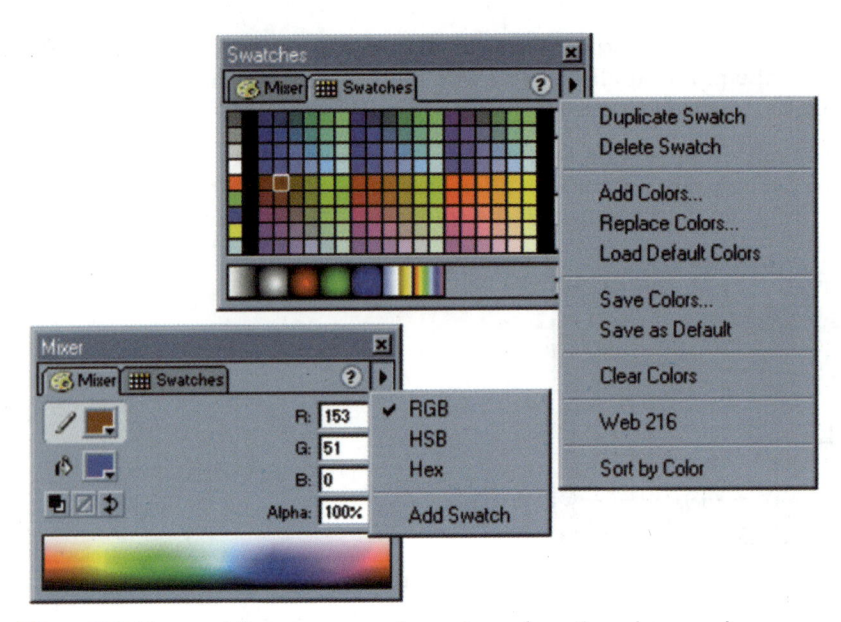

Figure 2.5 You can define your own colour scheme from the colour panels

Rectangle tool

Just as with the Oval tool, the **Rectangle** tool allows you to create rectangles either as outlines, fills or a combination of the two.

This time you will see that yet another icon is introduced within the set of rectangle modifiers. The last icon allows you to determine the shape of the corners. When you click on it, a **Rectangle Settings** dialog box appears allowing you to enter any number from 0 to 999 points (Figure 2.6).

2: Drawing and painting

*Just as with the keyboard shortcuts for Line (N) and Oval (O), you can access the Rectangle tool simply by keying **R** on your keyboard.*

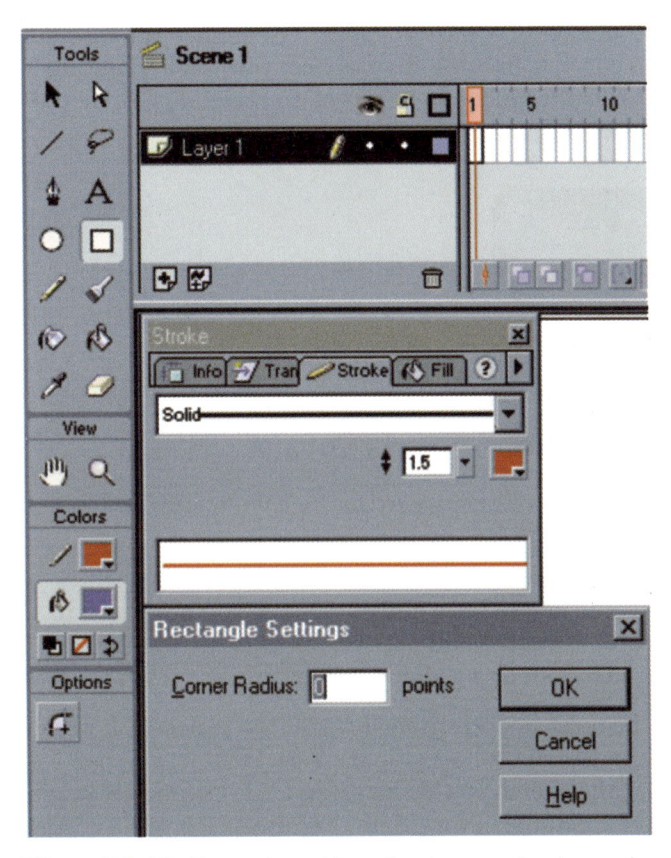

Figure 2.6 The Rectangle tool introduces yet another icon – the corner setting

A setting of 0 will give you perfectly square corners. The higher the number you enter, the rounder the corners become. In essence, what is happening is that the value that you enter is the radius in points of an imaginary circle that determines the rounded corner (Figure 2.7).

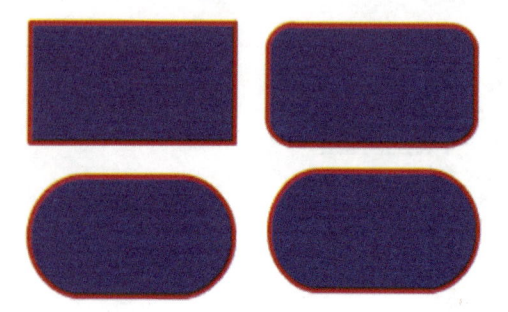

Figure 2.7 With the corner radius set to varying values, you can blunt the rectangle's corners

The pencil

When you use the **Pencil** tool to create lines and curves you can ask Flash to help you smooth out the wrinkles that will almost certainly occur whether you are using a mouse cursor, a rollerball or a graphics tablet for your input.

You do this using perhaps the most important modifier of the Pencil tool, which is found at the bottom of the pencil toolbar (Figure 2.8). With it, you can set your pencil to straighten out the sketch you make so that, for instance, a rough rectangle turns into a perfect rectangle every time (Figure 2.9); or a wavy line

*You can enter Pencil mode by keying **P** on your keyboard.*

can be turned into a smooth curve by selecting the Smooth option from the selector (Figure 2.10).

The degree of accuracy is set by opening the **Editing** dialog box from the **Edit:Preferences** menu and choosing from the selections on offer (Figure 2.11):

- **Connect lines** allows Flash to close open circles or rectangles.
- **Smooth curves** determines the degree of smoothing applied to a curve.
- **Recognize lines** determines how straight a line must be before Flash converts it to a straight line segment.
- **Recognize shapes** determines how close to a rectangle or ellipse a shape must be before Flash converts it to such an object.
- **Click accuracy** selects how close to a line segment you must be before Flash selects it.

There are also tick boxes, which allow you to determine the options for the **Pen** tool:

- Select **Show Pen Preview** to display a preview of the line segment as you move the pointer around the Stage, before you click to create the end point of the segment.
- Select **Show Solid Points** to specify that unselected anchor points appear as solid points (we'll be looking at selections in the next chapter).
- Select **Show Precise Cursors** to specify that the Pen tool pointer appears as a cross-hair pointer rather than the default Pen tool icon, for more precise placement of lines.

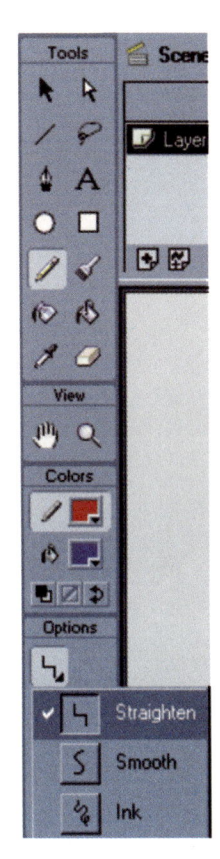

Figure 2.8 The Pencil tool

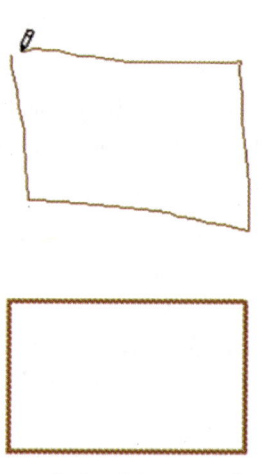

Figure 2.9 Straighten mode turns a rough sketch into a perfect rectangle

If you want to avoid these set defaults without having to go to the menu to switch everything off each time, you should choose **Ink Mode** from the Pencil

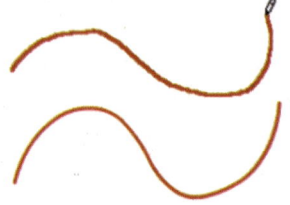

Figure 2.10 Smooth mode converts a wavy line into a smooth curve

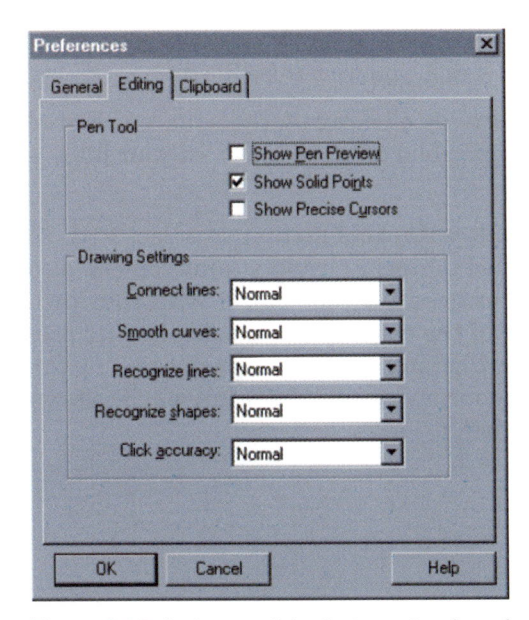

Figure 2.11 Each area of the Assistant is selected using the drop-down menus

mode selections. Now when you draw a shape, every judder, twist and turn will be reproduced faithfully.

Painting with the Paint Bucket
We've already seen how to fill an object with colour as we create it. But what if we want to fill the object later? This is where the **Paint Bucket** tool comes into

Flash 5 for Windows

its own (Figure 2.12). Select the Paint Bucket icon (or key **U** on the keyboard). You then click the mouse cursor inside the area you wish to be filled.

Once again you access the colour palette by clicking on the square coloured icon in the modifiers. As well as choosing a solid colour you can set your fill as a colour gradient (Figure 2.13).

This time you have to access the **Window:Panels** menu and select **Fill**. In Figure 2.13 you can see we have selected a Linear Gradient, but you can also choose to have a radial gradient fill, or even fill your object with your own chosen bitmap. Clicking on either end of the colour bar flags displays its present setting in the *Gradient Color* box. Clicking on this once will bring up the colour swatch for you to choose the appropriate colour; the result will be shown in the *Gradient preview* window to the left.

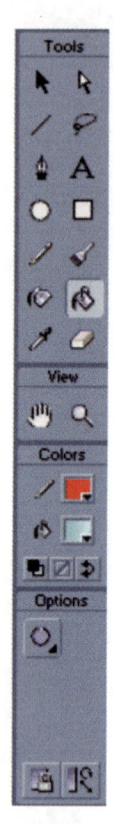

Figure 2.12 The Paint Bucket tool

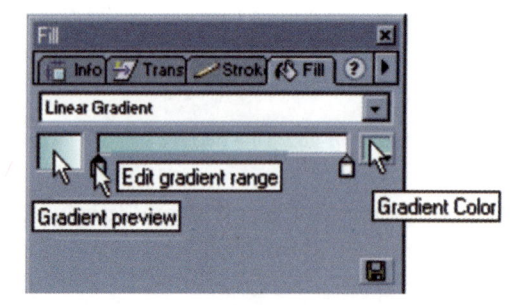

Figure 2.13 Creating a gradient fill

Once you have created your gradient, you may wish to alter the angle and size of gradient that is applied to your selection. This is applied with the **Transform Fill** button (the one on the bottom right in Figure 2.12). You can use the top (square) handle to resize horizontally; the middle (round) handle to resize in all directions; and the lower (round) handle to rotate the direction of fill (Figure 2.14).

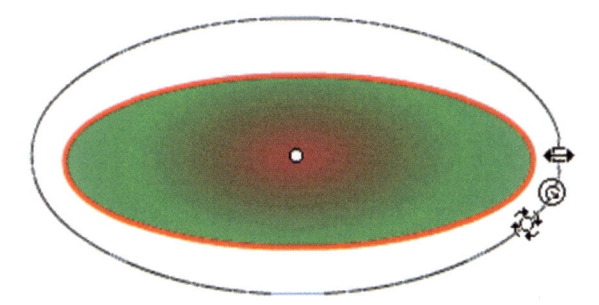

Figure 2.14 The size and angle of fill can be altered by dragging the modifier handles

Sometimes it happens that a shape you have created is not completely enclosed. Once again Flash comes to the rescue by making an intelligent guess as to whether you meant the shape to be enclosed or not. The **Gap Size** icon (immediately below **Options** in Figure 2.15) offers you a choice of 'closing' small, medium or large gaps.

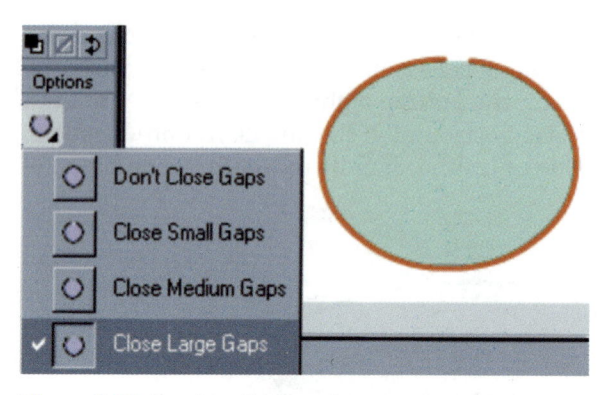

Figure 2.15 By asking Flash to close gaps for you, you can 'fill' an open shape

Painting with the Brush tool

Flash 5's **Brush** tool is used for creating flows of colour – fills with no outline, if you like. You can set the shape and size of the brush by clicking on the penultimate two icons shown in Figure 2.16.

Just below *Options* you will see an icon representing the Brush mode, which offers you various ways to interact with lines and shapes already on the Stage. Depending on the mode selected (Figure 2.17), the paint used by your Brush will affect or ignore particular areas of the Stage (Figure 2.18).

- **Paint Normal** paints over lines and fills, as long as they are on the same layer (we'll cover layers in Chapter 6).
- **Paint Fills** paints fills and empty areas, but does not paint over lines.
- **Paint Behind** paints only blank areas of the Stage. It leaves lines and fills unaffected.

Figure 2.16 The Paint Brush tool

2: Drawing and painting   33

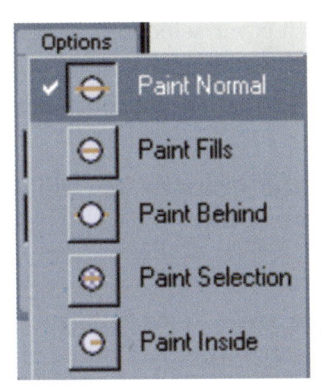

Figure 2.17 The Brush mode selector options

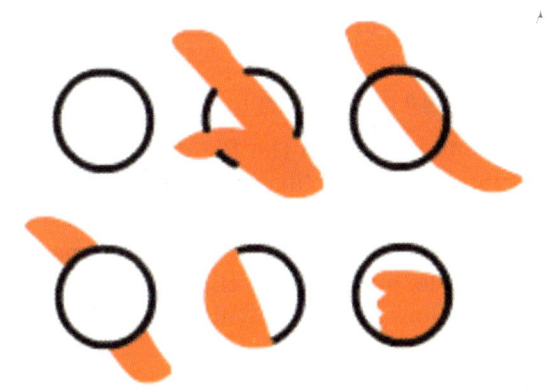

Figure 2.18 The Painting modes – Original Image, Paint Normal, Paint Fills, Paint Behind, Paint Selection, Paint Inside

- **Paint Selection** paints only over a selected fill (we'll cover selections in the next chapter).
- **Paint Inside** paints the fill area in which you start painting, but does not cross lines.

In a similar way to the Pencil Tool, if you hold down the **<Shift>** key while dragging a line, it forces it to go either horizontally or vertically.

The Eraser

Just as you can paint using the Paint Brush, so you can erase items from your Stage using the **Eraser**. You can select whether you want your eraser round or square, and in one of five sizes. You can erase in one of two ways:

1. By dragging using the settings offered in the Eraser mode dialog box. The size and shape of the eraser is set using the drop-down menu shown at the bottom of Figure 2.19.
2. By using the Faucet tool (which looks like a dripping tap).

With the former, you are offered a menu similar to the Paint Brush menu allowing you to determine whether you want to erase fills, lines, selected fills or whatever (Figure 2.20). When you use the Faucet tool, you click on the line or filled area that you want deleted. The little drip at the end of the tap marks the point at which your selections are made, but with one click you can erase an entire line or filled shape, regardless of how many segments go into making up the strokes.

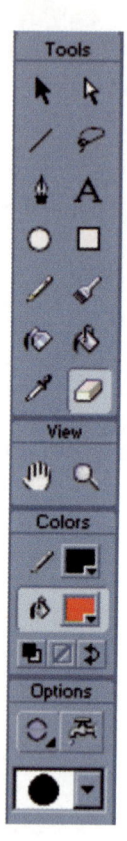

Figure 2.19 The Eraser tool with modifiers

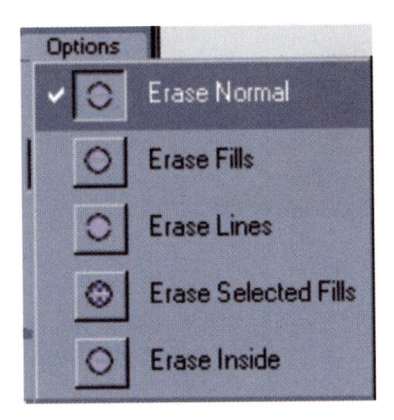

Figure 2.20 The Eraser mode menu selections

The Ink Bottle
You can apply an outline – a Stroke – to an area of fill colour by using the **Ink Bottle** tool (Figure 2.21).

Having selected the colour, width and style of stroke, click the Ink Bottle on an area as shown in Figure 2.22. As you can see, the fill outside the circle now has an outline to it, while the fill which is inside the circle is left alone. In other words, only the edge of the overall selection is given a new edge.

Well, that covers the basic creation of shapes and objects. Read on to see how you can make changes and improvements to what you've just done.

Figure 2.22 The Ink Bottle paints a stroke round an area of fill

Figure 2.21 The Ink Bottle tool with modifiers

Objects 3

Selecting objects
Repositioning
Simple editing commands
Resizing objects
Grouping objects

So far, we've concentrated – naturally enough – on creating objects. But it won't be long before you will want to alter your creations in some way.

Modifying objects is an all-encompassing term. It can include:

- moving
- colouring/re-colouring
- straightening
- smoothing
- scaling
- rotating
- and a whole lot more besides.

Selecting objects

The first step in changing an object is to make sure it is selected, and Flash 5 offers a variety of ways in which you can do this.

In common with most image-processing programs, you can use the arrow tool to click on an object to select it, but you can also select items by fully enclosing them, either using a rectangular selector or a free-form lasso.

We'll come to these methods in a moment. But because of the complex nature of many of the shapes you will be creating, it is necessary at this point to understand the way in which Flash 5 allows you to add to – or subtract from – your selections.

If you go to your **Edit** menu and select **Preferences:Clipboard**, you will see a dialog box like the one shown in Figure 3.1.

3: Objects 39

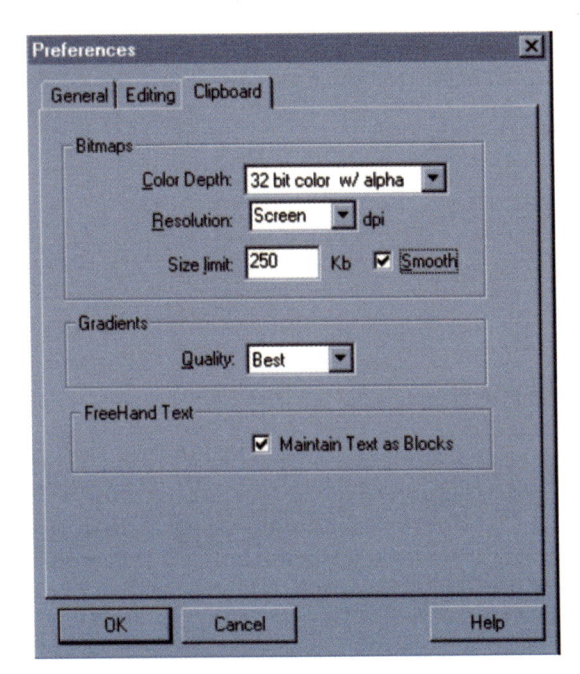

Figure 3.1 You set your select options from here

Selecting with the Arrow tool

The first thing to understand is that what you may regard as a straightforward and simple shape is not necessarily the way that Flash 5 treats it. Every time there is a twist or turn in a seemingly simple line, Flash defines a new vector path that then counts as a separate part of that line.

If, for instance, we draw a rectangle with rounded corners, Flash will treat it as four straight lines and four corners. In other words, a rectangle will be made up of eight vectors.

Figure 3.2 Hovering your cursor over a segment will show you what type it is

So let's make some selections. Select the **Arrow** tool from the Toolbar and move your mouse over your intended selection (Figure 3.2). The cursor will change into either a Curve point or a Corner point. By simply clicking on a segment, you can select it and the segment will become highlighted. At this point, the cursor changes once again, as you can see in Figure 3.3.

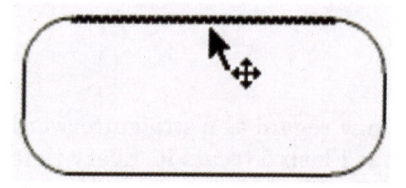

Figure 3.3 A selected segment with its associated cursor

To add another segment to your selection you need to hold down the **<Shift>** key as you select it. But if you want to select the entire shape, try double-clicking it instead. As long as all the segments are touching one another, the entire shape should become selected.

You can select a filled area in the same way you would select a line. With the Arrow tool you just click on it. The cursor changes into a selection arrow and the fill changes to a contrasting checkerboard pattern (Figure 3.4).

*If you are using another tool and you quickly want to select the Arrow tool, press the **<Ctrl>** key. The Arrow tool will remain your default as long as this is held down.*

Figure 3.4 Clicking the fill (left) creates a checkerboard pattern (right)

If you want to select a group of objects – lines, corners, fills and all – the quickest method is to use the Arrow tool to drag a rectangle over the objects to be selected. Releasing the mouse selects everything lying inside the rectangle.

Selecting with the Lasso tool

Using the Arrow tool and drawing out rectangles is a good way of selecting objects if there is enough room between them; but if objects are close together, a safer way of selecting them is to use the **Lasso** tool, which works in a similar way to most other image-processing programs.

*If you want to select everything on the Stage, you can go to the **Edit** menu and choose **Select All**. Or an even quicker method is to key **<Ctrl> A**.*

You don't need to close the Lasso selection if you are sure that the line that would have been drawn from your end point to your start point fully encloses your intended selection.

From the Toolbar, select the icon with the lasso on it, or simply press **L** on the keyboard. Holding down the mouse key, drag a freeform selection around the objects you wish to select and let go. Whatever is enclosed by the lasso will become selected.

For selecting really complex shapes it can prove difficult to hold down the mouse key and drag all round the objects. Instead, Flash offers you a method that will be kinder on your hand muscles! When you select the Lasso tool, you will see a set of modifier icons appear, the lowest of which is the **Polygon mode** icon (Figure 3.5).

If you select this before making your selection you will find that you can click your way around a shape adding segments as you go along. To close the selection process, double-click your mouse. You can even combine the two lasso operations by temporarily holding down the **<Alt>** key while using the Lasso – you will remain in Polygon mode for as long as you hold down the **<Alt>**.

Selecting portions

There are times when you will want to select only part of an element, and this is done using the Arrow or Lasso tools to enclose the areas in which you are interested (Figure 3.6)

Deselecting parts of a selection

We've seen how you can select objects in a variety of ways in Flash 5. Deselecting an object is much simpler. All you need to do is use the Arrow tool and **<Shift>**-click the partial selection.

3: Objects   43

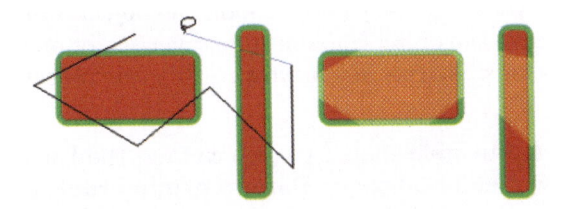

Figure 3.6 Selecting over the objects (left) creates a partial selection (right)

To deselect everything you can:

1. Go to the **Edit** menu and choose **Deselect All**.
2. Key **<Shift> <Ctrl> A** (all together).
3. Click in an empty area of your Stage.

So now that we've seen how to select and deselect items on our stage, the next question is: what can we do with our selections?

Repositioning

Once you have drawn an object, the chances are that you will want to position it accurately to line up with other items on your stage.

The quickest (and crudest) method is to click on the object with your arrow key and drag it to a new position. To help you position your object more accurately, you might care to switch on the rulers by going to your **View** menu and selecting **Rulers**. You could also switch on the positioning grid with **View:Grid: Show Grid**.

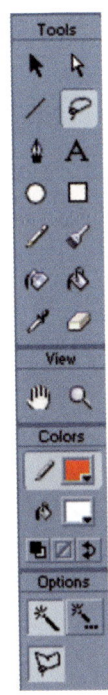

Figure 3.5 The Polygon mode icon is shown at the bottom of the lasso selection panel

For more accuracy you could select the arrow key and click on the object, but then use your four cursor keys to move the object horizontally or vertically, one pixel at a time. (If you hold down the **<Shift>** key as you do this, the object will move eight pixels at a time.)

If you want to specify exactly where your item should go, you can use the **Info panel** instead. Go to the **Window** menu and select **Panel:Info** in order to open a window similar to that shown in Figure 3.7.

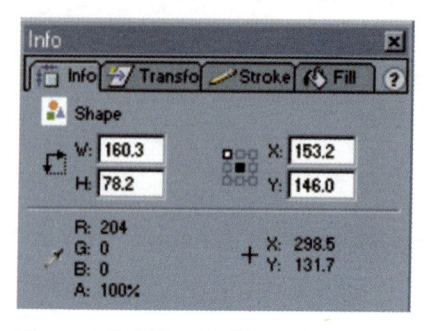

Figure 3.7 Using the Object Inspector to reposition your object

Here you can see that it is a simple matter of entering x and y co-ordinates for accurate placement of your object. The co-ordinate points refer to the top left-hand corner of the object's boundary. The Info panel also contains a small grid, with a black square that indicates the registration point. If the black square is not in the upper left corner of the grid, you can click the upper left square to move the registration point to that position.

Simple editing commands

In common with most Windows programs, Flash supports the standard Copy, Cut and Paste options. It also has a couple of aces up its sleeve to simplify the process further.

- To **Delete** a selection: select the elements you want to delete and press the **Delete** key (or go to the **Edit** menu and choose **Clear**). Flash removes your selection.
- To **Cut** a selection: select the elements and key **<Ctrl> X** (or **Edit** menu: **Cut**). The selection is copied to the Clipboard and removed from the Stage.
- To **Copy** a selection: select the elements and key **<Ctrl> C** (or **Edit** menu: **Copy**). The selection is copied to the Clipboard.
- To **Paste** the Clipboard contents to the centre of your current view, press **<Ctrl> V** (**Edit** menu: **Paste**).

Sometimes it will be important to paste the Clipboard contents in their original location – when you are creating multi-layered objects and exact positioning on another layer is crucial, for instance. For this version of pasting, key **<Ctrl> <Shift> V** or from your **Edit** menu select **Paste in Place**.

You can **Duplicate** an object by keying **<Ctrl> D** (or using the **Edit: Duplicate** menu). Although this doesn't change the contents of the Clipboard, it duplicates the original – offset – so that you can see both the original and the duplicate (Figure 3.8).

*Instead of using **Copy** and **Paste**, you can hold down the **<Ctrl>** key while dragging an object. A new copy of the item appears with the original left intact.*

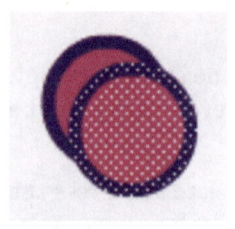

Figure 3.8 Duplicating a circle offsets the copy and selects it by default

There is one more Paste command – **Paste Special** – that we'll be looking at in Chapter 5 which allows you to paste in objects from other programs but which links the two. This allows you to edit the object in another program and immediately translate those changes to the object in Flash.

Changing line segments
Once drawn, you can use the Arrow tool to grab and reposition the end points of a straight line or curve. This allows you to lengthen or shorten them until they accurately reflect what you want. Flash also allows you to change the direction of a line segment by dragging the end of the line to a new position, or to change the direction of the end of a curve by dragging its end in a similar manner.

But you can also change the shape of a curve, or turn a straight line into a curve by grabbing a segment in the middle of a run and dragging it to a new position. Flash automatically redraws the curve (Figure 3.9).

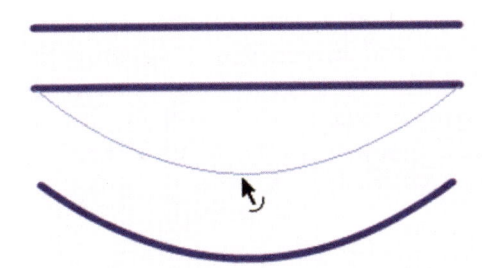

Figure 3.9 Dragging the centre of a straight line (top) until you get the outline you want (middle) creates a curve (bottom)

If you want to create a new corner point, rather than a curve, repeat the above but hold down the **<Ctrl>** key as you do it. The shape of the new curve will depend on the shape you started with, but with a little practice you will soon see what a powerful feature this is (Figure 3.10).

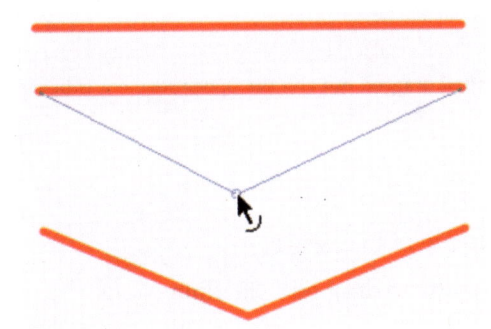

Figure 3.10 <Ctrl> dragging produces new corner points

Reshaping filled areas

Just as you can change the shapes of lines and curves, you can change the shape of a filled area. Although you can't see the edges of Fills, unless they have a stroked outline, they do nevertheless have their own (invisible) outlines. This means that you can select their curve points or corner points and distort them just as you would a stroked outline (Figure 3.11).

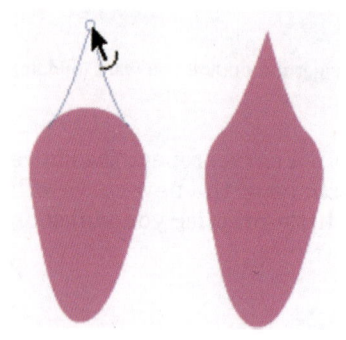

Figure 3.11 Here a circular fill has had its lower half dragged out and the upper segment is being given a new corner point drag

Resizing objects

Flash 5 enables you to resize an object in one of four ways:

1. You can use the **Arrow** tool in resize mode to drag out the dimensions.
2. You can apply a **Scale** command.

3: Objects

3. You can use the **Info panel**.
4. You can use the **Panel:Transform Inspector**.

Figure 3.12 The resize icon

1. With your object selected, click on the resize icon to give your selection some resizing handles (Figure 3.12). By dragging out the central handles, you can resize either horizontally or vertically (Figure 3.13). Dragging one of the corner handles, on the other hand, resizes in both directions so that your aspect ratio remains the same.

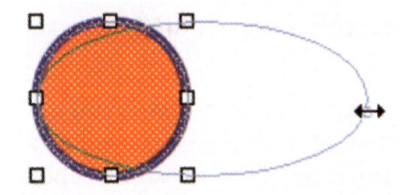

Figure 3.13 Resizing horizontally

2. To resize an object using the Scale command, go to the **Modify** menu and choose **Transform:Scale and Rotate**. If you add a percentage greater than 100, the object will be uniformly magnified. To reduce its size, however, you enter a number less than 100 (Figure 3.14).

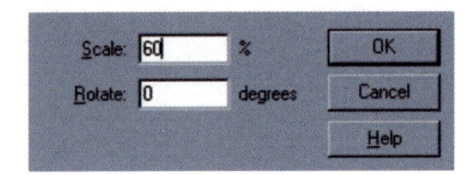

Figure 3.14 Using the Scale and Rotate menu

3. When we considered repositioning an object earlier on, we saw that one can use the **Info panel** to enter co-ordinates (Figure 3.7). You can use this same tool to enter width and height settings – remembering that if you want to scale an object proportionally then this is not the tool for you! Each setting has to be entered by you, so if you want automatic scaling, use the **Transform Inspector**...

4. You can access the **Transform panel** by going to the **Window** menu and choosing **Panels:Transform**. Having selected your object, you need to ✔ the check box labelled **Constrain** if you want your object resized proportionally and then enter the percentage increase or decrease in the **Scale** boxes (Figure 3.15). Press **Enter** to make the changes.

3: Objects   51

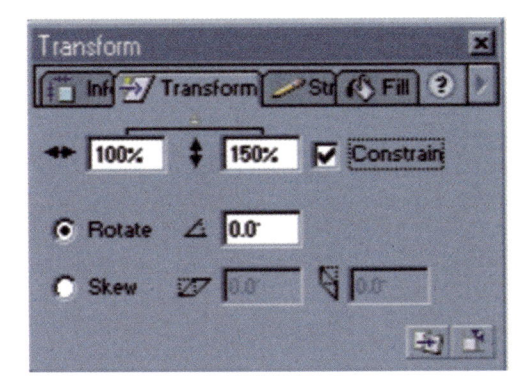

Figure 3.15 Using the Transform panel to resize an object

If you want to resize several objects at once, make your selections first and then use any of the above four methods to convert them as one batch.

Changing an object's orientation

In common with most imaging programs, Flash 5 allows you to **flip**, **skew** or **rotate** an object, but once again the software comes up with a variety of ways in which you can do so. The quickest (and crudest) way is to use the **Rotate** icon on your tool bar and then to use the 'handles' attached to your selection outlines to either rotate or skew the object. In Figure 3.16, for instance, an object is selected and the rotate icon selected, which produces an outline with 'handles' (top right). Dragging one of the corner handles rotates the object (bottom left), while grabbing one of the centre handles skews the object (bottom right).

If, instead of using the rotate icon you use the resize icon next to it (Figure 3.12), you can **flip** the object – either horizontally or vertically – by grabbing one of the

Flash 5 for Windows

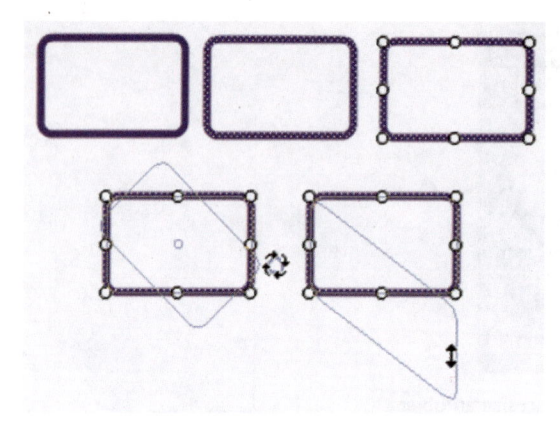

Figure 3.16 Rotating and skewing using the object's rotation handles

resulting handles and dragging it right out to the other side of the bounding box. The flipped object starts small but grows as you continue to drag away from the bounding box.

You can rotate objects easily, either in 90-degree steps (from the **Modify** menu choose **Transform:Rotate CW** [clockwise] – or **CCW** [anti-clockwise]) or by specified amounts by selecting **Modify:Transform:Scale and Rotate** which will give you a dialog box as in Figure 3.14 and you can just enter the degree of rotation.

Similarly, you can use the **Transform panel** that we saw in Figure 3.15 to set the amount of skew.

Alignment

When we move on to animation techniques in Chapter 8 it will become apparent just how important it is to be able to align individual items together on the Stage. Flash 5 allows you to align selected objects along their tops, bottoms, sides or centres.

You can even resize one object to match the dimensions of another so that they are all the same width, or height, or whatever.

You access the **Align panel** from the Window menu in the normal way, or by keying **<Ctrl> K** (Figure 3.17).

Figure 3.17 The Align panel dialog box

Having selected the objects you want aligned, you can choose to align them vertically or horizontally via their midpoints or by either edge, as well as determining the spacing between each. The icons within the alignment dialog box are pretty clear at showing you what is on offer. You can also **distribute** selected objects so that their centres or edges are evenly spaced. The **Match Size** option allows you to match horizontally, vertically or proportionally with one another.

Select **To Stage** to apply alignment modifications relative to the overall Stage dimensions.

Grouping objects

As you work with a number of objects on your Stage, the time will come when you will want to regard groups of individual objects as a single object in their own right. Flash allows you to group these selected objects together by going to the **Modify** menu and selecting **Group**.

Once grouped, they behave like any other single object, except that the group that you last created will be given priority in terms of appearing at the top of the 'stack' of visible objects. In other words, if you have two groups of objects that overlap, the one that was created last will appear on top of the older group.

If, having created a group, you wish to make changes to one element within the group, you can edit it by double-clicking on the grouped item, and a flag appears in the top left corner of the Stage informing you that you are no longer editing directly onto the Stage but instead within the group only (Figure 3.18).

You can change the visibility order by simply selecting ***Modify:Arrange:Send to Back*** *(or* ***Bring to Front****) so that different grouped elements have priority.*

Figure 3.18 The Group 'flag' shows you are no longer editing the Scene

When you have finished making changes to your grouped item, click once again on the **Scene** 'flag' to the left of the Group 'flag' to return to normal editing mode.

Type 4

Inserting text
Setting type attributes
Transforming type
Converting type

Inserting text

As well as placing objects on your Stage, you will almost certainly want to use text in one form or another within your Flash environment.

The text tool – represented by a capital 'A' – together with its modifiers, is what you will use initially for inserting text into your work. You can place type on a single line that expands as you type or in a fixed-width block that wraps words automatically.

Begin by clicking on the text tool icon and then click once anywhere on the Stage. A small box will appear with a round circle in its top right-hand corner. Start typing and you'll see that the box expands to contain the available text (Figure 4.1).

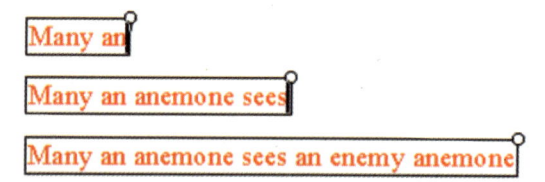

Many an

Many an anemone sees

Many an anemone sees an enemy anemone

Figure 4.1 The round handle in the top right corner shows there is no wrap switched on. Note how the text box expands to accommodate the text

To create a text block with a fixed width, however, you first need to position the pointer where you want the text to start and then drag out the box to the desired width. Instead of a circle being displayed at the top right end of the box, you should have a little square, which denotes a fixed width. Now when you type, the paragraph will automatically wrap itself round to the next line rather than push out the limits of the box (Figure 4.2).

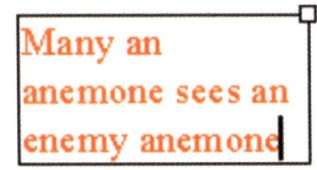

Figure 4.2 The square handle shows that the width has been fixed

Another way to set a finite width is to start with an expandable box, as before, but then to drag the round handle to the desired width. The round handle will turn square and a finite width will be created.

Setting type attributes

Setting the weight and style of a font is comparable to that in most desktop publishing (DTP) and word-processing packages. You can set the attributes before you start typing text, or highlight text that you want to change in some way and then set its attributes.

Using the **Character panel**, select the font you want, together with its size, whether you want it bold and/or italic, whether it should be *normal* text, *Superscript* or *subscript*, and whether you want the horizontal spacing of the letters stretched out (ie *tracking*) or *kerned* (Figure 4.3). You can also set the colour of the font in this manner.

There is another type of text field box used for interactive and dynamic text, which we shall look at in Chapter 9.

Kerning controls the spacing between pairs of characters. Many fonts have built-in kerning information. For example, the spacing between an A and a V is often less than the spacing between an A and a D.

*A faster way of accessing the Character panel is to click on the '**A**' icon at the bottom right hand corner of the Flash Stage area.*

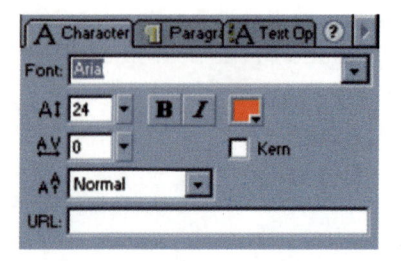

Figure 4.3 Set the text formatting options from the Character panel

When selecting your text, Flash displays what it looks like so that you can make your choice easily (Figure 4.4). But you also have the option of using one of the device fonts on offer. It's very important to appreciate the difference between embedded fonts and device fonts. When you use a font installed on your system, Flash embeds the font information in the final Flash player (SWF, or shockwave format) file, ensuring that the font displays properly in the Flash Movie.

*Not all fonts displayed in Flash can be exported with a movie. To verify that a font can be exported, use the **View:Antialias Text** command to preview the text; jagged type indicates that Flash does not recognise that font's outline and will not export the text.*

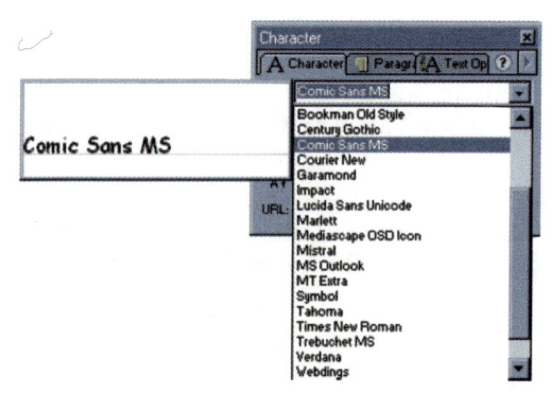

Figure 4.4 Flash does its best to help you make your design decisions

As an alternative to embedding font information, you can use the **device fonts** that come with Flash. Device fonts are not embedded in the Flash SWF file. Instead, the Flash Player uses whatever font on the local computer most closely resembles the device font. Because device font information is not embedded, using device fonts yields a somewhat smaller Flash movie file size. In addition, at small type sizes (typically below 10 points), device fonts can be sharper and more legible than embedded fonts. However, if users do not have a font installed on their system that corresponds to the device font, type may appear very different from that which you have designed.

The three device fonts included with Flash are **_sans** (similar to Arial), **_serif** (similar to Times Roman), and **_typewriter** (similar to Courier).

You can also set the paragraph attributes, much as you would in any word-processing program (Figure 4.5). Click on the **Paragraph panel** to adjust:

- left and right margins;
- the amount of indentation for the first line of text;
- the spacing between lines;
- alignment of text (left, right, centre or fully justified).

Remember, though, that unless you show the borders of your text field in your final presentation, your audience will not be aware of the size of your margins. However, this facility may well be useful if you intend this text to be editable in the final presentation (see Chapter 9).

Flash uses point size when determining the spacing between lines of text and pixels for the margin settings. Unlike previous versions of Flash, you cannot enter the wrong units by mistake.

Flash 5 for Windows

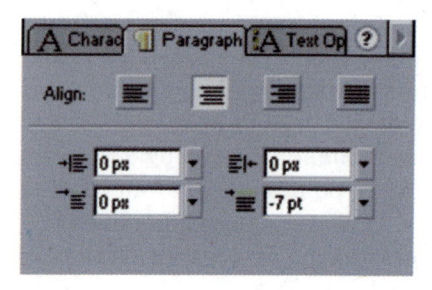

Figure 4.5 The Paragraph panel dialog box

When you scale a text block as an object, increases or decreases in point size are not reflected in the Character panel.

Transforming type

You can transform text blocks in the same way as other objects; that is, you can scale, rotate, skew and flip text blocks to create some interesting effects (Figure 4.6). The text in a transformed text block can still be edited, although be wary of going mad with your designs as severe transformations can make the text difficult to read.

Figure 4.6 Has Naomi finally flipped? Rotation and skew work on text just as they do on any object

Converting type

There will be occasions when, having written text into your movie, you will want to work with it just as if it was any other object, so that you can stretch it, distort it and paint it for instance.

To convert your text to such an object, select it and then go to your **Modify** menu. Choose **Break Apart**. Break Apart applies only to outline fonts such as TrueType fonts. Bitmap fonts disappear from the screen when you break them apart.

Having converted your font to an object, you can then manipulate it any way you like (Figure 4.7). Remember that it's too late now to go back and edit your text!

You can only convert an entire block of text at one time; individual characters cannot be converted by themselves. Once you have converted type to line strokes and fills, you will no longer be able to edit your text.

Figure 4.7 Once you've broken apart your text, you can treat it just like any other object

We'll be examining the use of text as objects in much more detail in Chapter 7.

Imported artwork 5

Using imported graphics in Flash
Acceptable file formats
Converting bitmaps to vector elements
Painting with a bitmapped image
Using the Magic Wand

Using imported graphics in Flash

As well as enabling you to produce quite complex graphics, Flash 5 allows you to import graphics from other programs. This gives you the option of producing something using advanced features in another package and then using them within Flash.

When importing graphic elements, you can import both vector graphics and raster – or bitmapped – images. So if you already use image-processing applications such as Freehand, Illustrator, Paint Shop Pro or CorelDraw, you can rest assured that it is likely you will be able to utilise any existing artwork.

Flash 5 can also import movie files, and we'll return to this later.

Acceptable file formats

If you want hassle-free translation from another vector program into Flash 5, the best way is to import graphics as .swf (Shockwave format) files. For example, Freehand (another program from the Macromedia stable) can accept most vector formats from other programs and resave them as .swf files. These files have the advantage of containing gradient and vector layers intact, whereas Flash may not cope with gradients in other formats too well. You could of course always recreate the gradients using Flash's own tools, but that rather defeats the object, doesn't it?

Not everyone has Freehand, of course. If you have Adobe Illustrator, then Flash 5 recognises 88, 3.0, 5.0 and 6.0 formats. Although Flash can read .eps files created by Illustrator, it might have difficulty with .eps files created by other applications.

Be aware that, although you can import most vector graphics, you may find that not all the features of other vector-producing applications translate readily into Flash.

Other file types that are supported are:
- .emf (enhanced metafile)
- .wmf (Windows metafile)
- .dxf (AutoCAD)
- .bmp (Windows bitmap)
- .gif (Compuserve graphic image format)
- .jpg (JPEG)
- .png (Portable Network Graphics)
- .spl (FutureSplash).

Flash 5 can also import some extra file formats if you have QuickTime 4 or later installed on your system. This could be especially useful if you work on both Windows and Macintosh platforms. With QuickTime 4 you can import:

- .psd (Adobe Photoshop)
- .pic (PICT)
- .tif (TIFF)
- .tga (Targa)
- .sai (Silicon Graphics)
- .mov (QuickTime Movie).

Importing raster graphics
Raster graphics can easily be brought into the Flash environment by going to your **File** menu and selecting **Import**, which gives you an Import dialog box as in Figure 5.1.

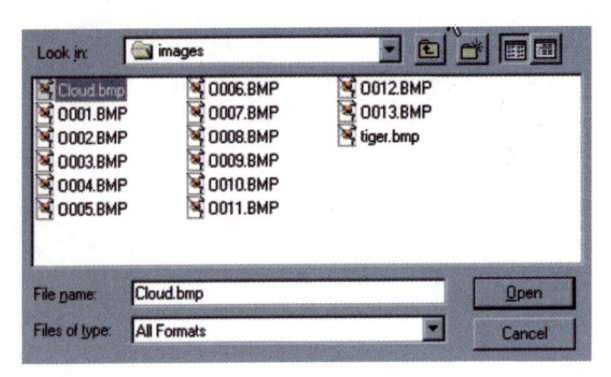

Figure 5.1 The Import dialog box

You navigate in the normal way to the particular file on your computer system and either click on **Open** or double-click on the file in question. Flash responds by storing a copy of the bitmap in question on the Stage in whatever layer is currently active (see Chapter 6) as well as placing a copy of it in its library (see Chapter 7).

Sometimes you will want to import a number of sequential files for use as keyframes in a movie. (We'll cover keyframes in Chapter 8). If all the file names are identical (such as in Figure 5.1), apart from a series of sequential numbers, Flash will ask you if you want to import all, rather than just one, image (Figure 5.2).

Importing vector-based graphics
Importing vector graphics is a very similar process to that used for raster graphics. The main difference lies in what Flash does with the file.

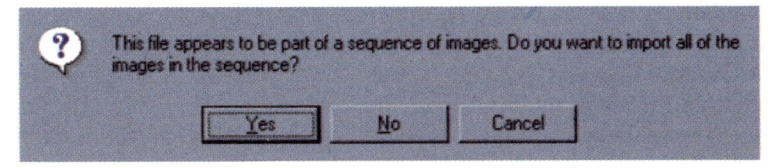

Figure 5.2 Flash recognises a sequence of files, and offers to import them all for you

When importing vector files from Adobe Illustrator and from Macromedia Fireworks, the original layers are recreated within Flash.

Whereas a bitmapped image is placed both on the Stage and in the Library, a vector image is placed on the Stage as a grouped object but it is not placed in the Library. You can **ungroup** the vector image (by choosing **Modify: Ungroup**), allowing you to work with the ungrouped object much as you would with any vector image created within Flash itself.

Importing via the Clipboard

Both bitmaps and vector images can be pasted into Flash via Windows' Clipboard. It's a little bit hit and miss, however, as vector objects in particular can lose some of their information, leading to oddities in the translation. But as a 'quick and dirty' method it is very simple.

Start by opening up the application used to create the graphic and select and copy the object (very often, though not always, using **<Ctrl> C**). Open up Flash (if it is not already open) or click anywhere within the Flash environment to 'bring it alive' and click **<Ctrl> V** or **Edit:Paste.**

Once again, if the object is a bitmapped image, it will be placed both on the Stage and in the Library, while if it is a vector image it will be placed purely on the Stage.

Flash also has an import option, which is known as *Paste Special*. This differs from the previous use of the Clipboard in that, instead of pasting the contents directly onto the Stage, Flash pastes them at the same time as creating links to the original files. If you want to modify these items, Flash will then open up the original program where you can make your changes; anything that you then change will be reflected in the image on Flash's stage.

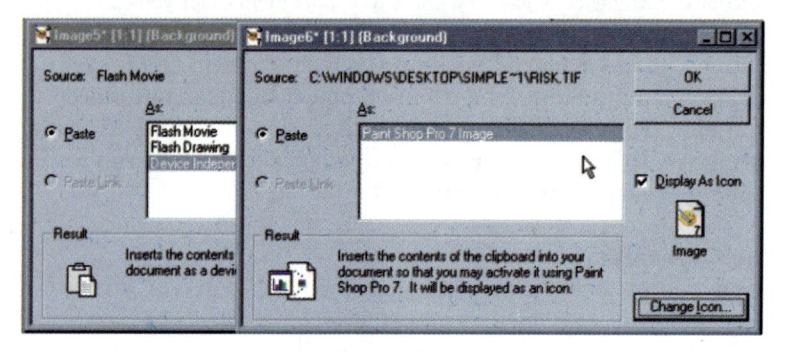

Figure 5.3 The Paste Special dialog box, which changes depending on what is in the Clipboard

In Figure 5.3 you can see that you are sometimes given the option of which format you would like to paste your file. For example, TIFF files on this occasion are recognised as 'belonging' to JASC's Paint Shop Pro.

Converting bitmaps to vector elements

You can convert a bitmapped image into a vector file, allowing you to work on the image in exactly the same way you would any other vector object. Because photographic-type images could well end up with a massive amount of colour shadings and vector curves, it is necessary to strike a happy balance between accuracy and file manageability.

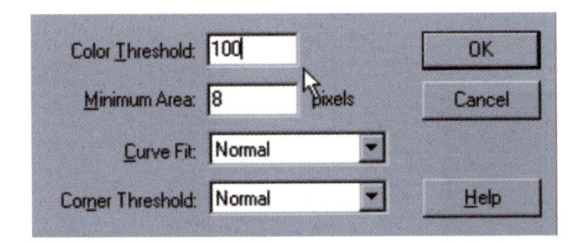

Figure 5.4 The Trace Bitmap dialog box

With the bitmapped image on your Stage, select **Modify:Trace Bitmap** from the file menu and a dialog box similar to that shown in Figure 5.4 will appear. As you can see, there are a number of parameters you can enter and they control how close a match your final vector image will be to the original bitmapped image.

- **Color Threshold** determines the amount of similar colours that get clumped together within one vector object. With a low threshold, more individual colours are recognised, but the downside to this is that you end up with many more vector objects and a correspondingly larger file size.
- **Minimum Area** guides Flash into working with neighbouring pixels to work out a colour match. The more pixels it works with, the lower the detail and the lower the file size.

70 Flash 5 for Windows

- **Curve Fit** determines the smoothness of the curved outlines around individual vector shapes.

- **Corner Threshold** tells Flash whether it should create sharp corners or more rounded ones.

Although Macromedia recommends that settings for photographs should be 'Color Threshold, 10; Minimum Area, 1; Curve Fit, pixels; Corner Threshold, Many corners', you are likely to end up with huge files if you follow this advice. Ask yourself why you would want to have this level of resolution in your vector object and see if you cannot find a way around it – perhaps by combining a vector and a bitmapped graphic so that only the area that needs to be vectorised is converted (compare Figure 5.5 and 5.6).

Figure 5.5 A picture of a tiger, traced with a *color threshold* of 10 and a *minimum* area of 1

Figure 5.6 The same picture traced with a *color threshold* of 50 and a *minimum* area of 20

Painting with a bitmapped image

Bitmapped images can be used to fill other areas as a repeating pattern. You might find this useful if, for instance, you wanted to fill some text with an image pattern, or wanted to 'paint' the pattern onto the side of an object.

First we select the bitmapped image on your Stage. Let's use a sunset to superimpose on some objects (Figure 5.7).

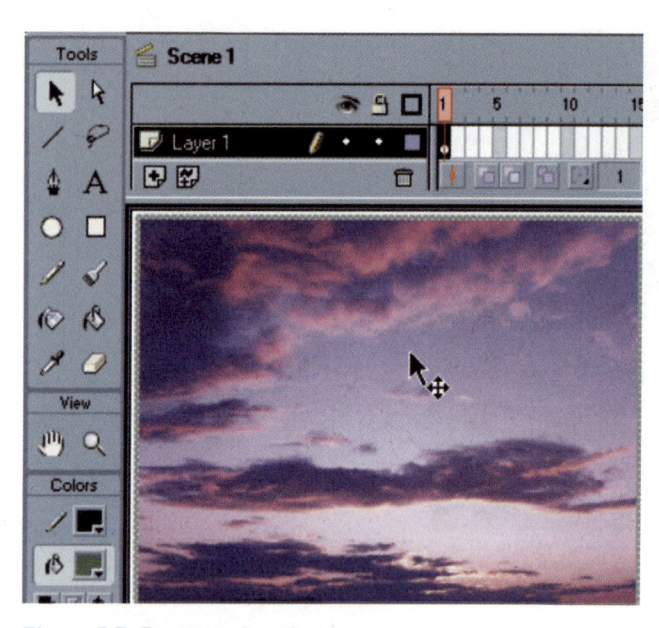

Figure 5.7 First we select the bitmap

From the **Modify** menu select **Break Apart**. You will see that the entire bitmapped image looks as if it is covered by a tiny grid, similar to that shown in Figure 5.8. If you now select the dropper tool and click anywhere on the 'broken apart' image it will select it as a fill pattern so that it can be used in a similar way to a gradient fill.

Figure 5.8 The bitmap is 'broken apart' waiting for the dropper tool

You will see that the paint bucket tool has been automatically selected, and that the fill colour icon in the modifier palette is filled with a tiny representation of the image (Figure 5.9). You could use this image to fill a selected area of an object. Alternatively, you could try using the paint brush or create filled rectangles and ellipses to see the power of the software in action (Figure 5.10).

Once you have filled your object, you might decide that you want the focus of the fill altered. Perhaps you want another part of the fill as the focus, or you want it resized. To move the centre of a bitmapped fill, select the paint bucket tool and then choose the **transform fill** modifier (Figure 5.11).

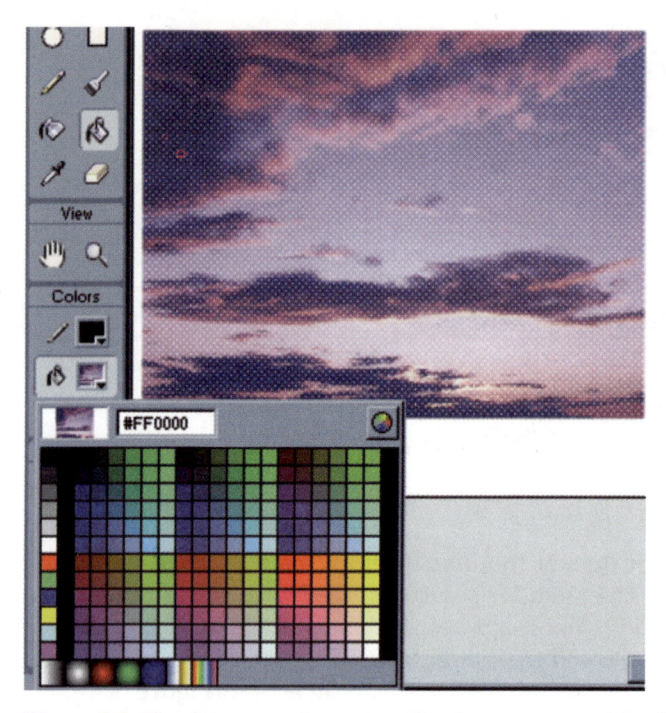

Figure 5.9 The dropper tool is replaced by the paint pot and the fill colour is replaced by the image

Figure 5.10 Filling and painting areas with our original image

Figure 5.11 The Transform Fill modifier icon

If you position the resulting cursor over your fill object and click, you will see handles for manipulating the object appear. You use:

- the central handle to reposition the centre of the fill;
- the bottom or top handle to alter the height of the fill;

- the side handles to alter its width;
- the bottom left corner handle to alter the size proportionally;
- the top right corner handle to rotate the object.

Using the Magic Wand

You can use the **Magic Wand** tool to select areas of a bitmapped image that have like colours. For instance, on the picture of the sunset that we have been using we might want to select a patch of dark sky.

First you need to select the bitmapped image as before and break it into its component colours (**Modify:Break Apart**). Unselect the image.

Now choose the **Lasso** tool and select the **Magic Wand Modifier**. By clicking on particular colours of the image with your magic wand you can select whole areas of like colour (Figure 5.12).

If you want to, you can then modify that particular area, such as painting it with solid colour using the bucket fill or even deleting portions of it so that a lower level of design comes through the 'holes' in the picture.

You can alter the magic wand's settings by clicking on the right-hand modifier. Here you can set the threshold and the smoothing levels as before.

5: Imported artwork 77

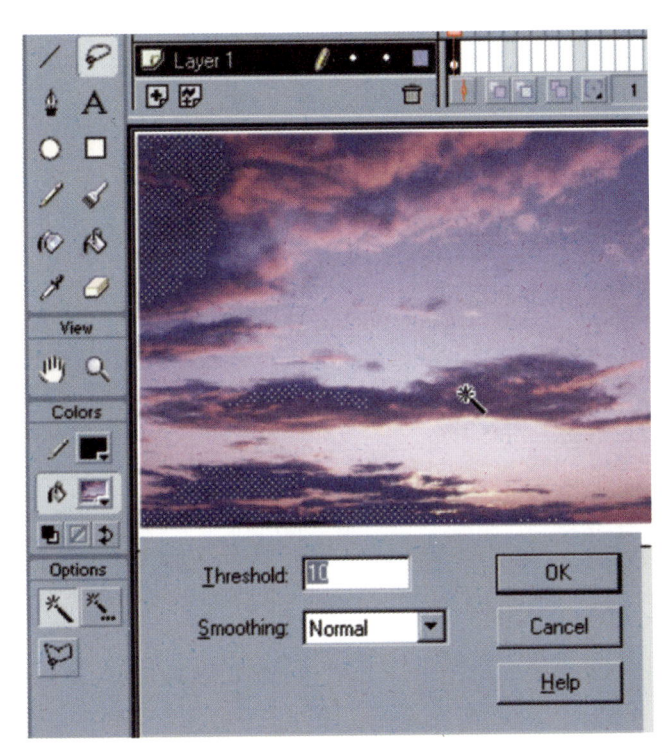

Figure 5.12 Using the magic wand you can select an entire area of like colours

Layers 6

Creating and deleting layers
Using the Layers dialog box
Using the Timeline to control layers
Stacking objects on different layers
Guide layers
Mask layers
Paste in place

Importing and creating artwork in Flash is all very well, but very quickly you could get to the point where the workings on one section of your artwork could interfere with other aspects of your image creation. In addition, the more images that are stacked one on top of the other, the more complicated the manipulating of those images becomes.

Flash, in common with many other image creation programs, uses **Layers** to circumvent this problem. Think of a pad made up of a number of sheets of tracing paper, but instead of being translucent, you can see clearly through each one. Each sheet has a separate part of the image you are working on and you can arrange for separate sheets to hide or display the work underneath their own. You can move the layers around in any order and you can move the objects within each layer.

The main power of layers lies in the fact that you can edit or manipulate the objects on a particular layer without affecting any of the objects on other layers; or, in addition, you can get the objects on one particular layer to affect the objects on another layer in some predetermined way.

And when it comes to animating your movie, layers really come into their own by providing the facility to move objects along predefined paths. We'll deal with animation in Chapter 8.

Flash gives a visual representation of each layer at the start of the Timeline. When you start up Flash there will, of course, be only one layer since you have yet to create any. You can see in Figure 6.1 that there is a selection of icons associated with the layer Timeline. We'll come to the use of the top three icons in a short while. For the moment, though, you will notice two icons in the bottom left-hand corner which are used for creating *new layers* and *new guide layers* respectively. On the bottom right-hand side is a dustbin (or trash can) icon used for *deleting* layers.

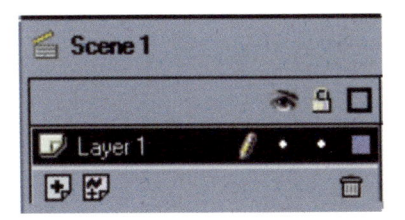

Figure 6.1 Flash begins with one layer

You will also see that, by default, Flash has called your base layer *'Layer 1'*. As each new layer is created, it will be given a number equivalent to the number of new layers created (not necessarily the number of layers in existence, since you might have deleted or merged some).

You can easily rename these layers and, in fact, it is probably best to do so since as you create more and more layers it is easy to lose track of where you are. To rename a layer, simply double-click on the name and type in a new one.

There is another way to rename your layer, and that is via the **Layer Properties** dialog box. We'll be returning to this dialog box throughout this chapter. To access it, go to your **Modify** menu and click on **Layer**, or right-click on the layer itself and choose **Properties**, or double-click on either the **sheet** icon (next to 'Layer 1' in Figure 6.1) or the **solid square** icon at the right-hand end of the 'Layer 1' layer. The dialog box will be similar to that shown in Figure 6.2.

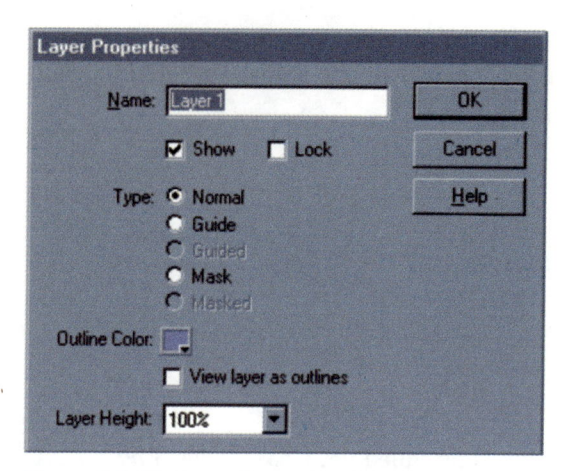

Figure 6.2 The Layer Properties dialog box

The first field is where you can type in a name for the layer. In fact, when the box appears, you will see the name is already highlighted, waiting for you to type in your new name straight away.

Creating and deleting layers

It is normal to create layers on the fly as you need them, although there is no reason why you could not create a number of layers to start off with and then work on them individually after that.

You can create layers in a number of ways. The simplest is to click on the '+' icon at the bottom left of the Timeline that we saw in Figure 6.1. However, you could also **Insert** a **Layer** from the menu bar (Figure 6.3) or even key **<Alt> I**, **<Alt> L**.

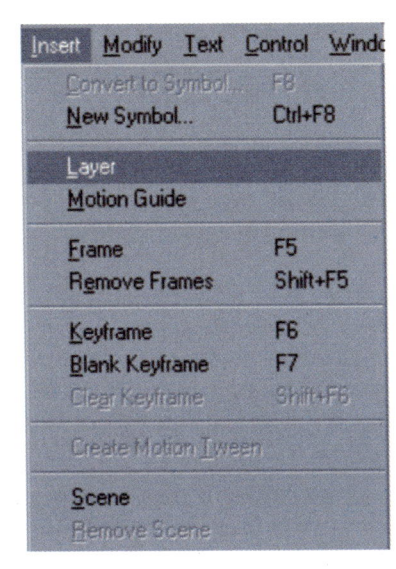

Figure 6.3 Inserting a new layer via the menu bar

Flash will always create a new layer above the currently selected one, so it is important to think where in the stacking order you want your new layer to appear. Which is the current layer? If you look at Figure 6.1 you will see that Layer 1 has a black background, as well as having a pencil icon (we'll return to that pencil in a moment). All the layers that are not the currently selected one will have a blue or grey background.

If you want to delete more than one layer at a time, make a selection of layers together holding down the <Ctrl> key as you do so, and then click on the dustbin.

Deleting a layer is just as easy. Either select the layer by clicking on it and then drag it to the dustbin or just click on the dustbin with the layer selected. Alternatively, **right-click** on the layer itself and select **Delete Layer**.

Using the Layers dialog box

We saw in Figure 6.2 that you can use the Layers dialog box to rename a particular layer. It can also be used to set other parameters for that layer.

Visibility
For instance, when you have objects on many layers, it sometimes gets confusing to have all the layers visible on the stage at once when trying to tweak one small aspect of a particular object. To aid you in your editing, you can make any of the layers temporarily invisible so that they don't get in the way of the object you are trying to see.

You will see in Figure 6.2 that the second row has two tick boxes. If the **Show** box has a tick, the layer will be visible; no tick, and the layer will become invisible.

Locking
Similarly, once you have worked on an object you may wish to protect it from accidental changes made when editing another object. In this instance, if you tick the **Lock** box, it will protect that layer from any further changes. When the layer is locked, you can still see the objects but you cannot select them or edit them.

Outline colours
You will see that one of the options allows you to view the contents of a layer as a set of outlines and to change the outline colour. In order to aid the placing of

objects on the stage relative to one another, Flash gives you the option of displaying purely the outlines of objects. To do so, tick the check box marked **View layer as outlines**.

So that you can determine which outlines are on which layers, you can colour-code the outlines so that, for instance, the outlines of objects on layer 1 could be in red, layer 2 in green, and so on. Clicking on the coloured rectangle next to **Outline Color** will bring up a colour palette from which you can choose whichever colour you wish (Figure 6.4).

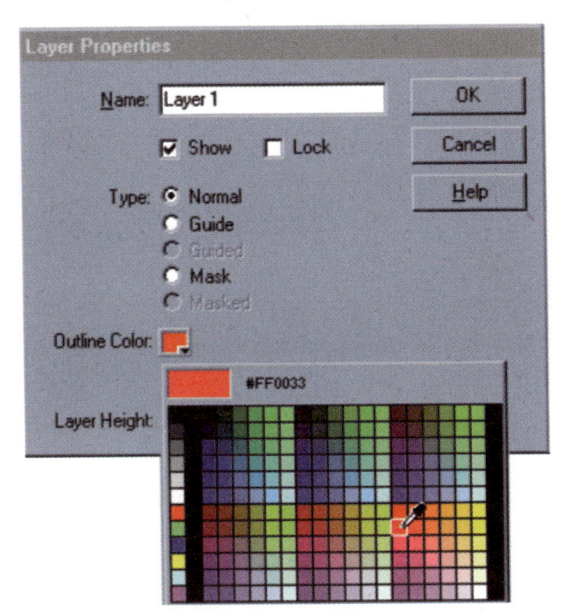

Figure 6.4 Changing the outline colours of your wire frames

Changing a layer's height

The lowest box in the Layer Properties dialog box allows you to alter the height of the layer bars in the Timeline. This is especially useful if you want to view the waveforms of sound channels, which are hard to see at the normal 100% setting (see Chapter 10).

Changing the type of layer

You will have noticed that the middle of the Layer Properties dialog box is taken up with a series of radio buttons allowing you to determine the type of layer you wish to work on.

You can set a layer as:

- Normal
- Guide
- Guided
- Mask
- Masked.

In addition, a layer can be a Motion Guide layer, which we will look at in Chapter 8.

- The **Normal** layer is the default, and all objects in a normal layer will appear in your final movie.
- **Guide** layer objects do not appear in a final movie. They are there purely to guide objects on other layers to be positioned accurately, or to move in a particular direction or path.

- A **Guided** layer is aligned to a guide layer and reacts according to its settings.
- A **Mask** layer can either hide or reveal the contents of layers lying below in the stacking order.
- These lower layers are called **Masked** layers.

In the Timeline, these different layers are shown with different label icons, as shown in Figure 6.5.

Figure 6.5 Each type of layer has its own individual icon

Using the Timeline to control layers

Many of the controls we talked about in the previous section can be more easily achieved by clicking on icons in the Timeline.

If you look at Figure 6.6, you will see three icons in the top right-hand corner, which are, respectively:

1. Visibility
2. Locking
3. Outlines.

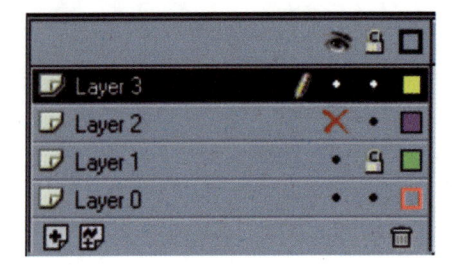

Figure 6.6 Control icons in the Timeline

If you click on a bullet below the 'eye' icon, the bullet will turn into a red cross sign, and that layer will no longer be visible.

Click on a bullet below the padlock icon, and the bullet turns into a padlock. Now, any objects on that particular layer are protected from being edited.

A click on a filled square below the square icon itself turns into an empty square, leaving all objects in that layer shown as outlines only. The colour of the square is representative of the colour of the layer's outlines.

If you want to change the visibility, lock or outline properties of a number of consecutive layers in one go, click a bullet on the first layer and drag the mouse button through all the other layers.

Stacking objects on different layers

When you place objects on different layers, those in the higher layer levels will always appear 'on top' of the lower objects.

Suppose you have three shapes – a lozenge, a square and a circle placed on three layers, 3, 2 and 1 respectively. As you will see in Figure 6.7, the square is placed over the circle, while both are eclipsed by the lozenge.

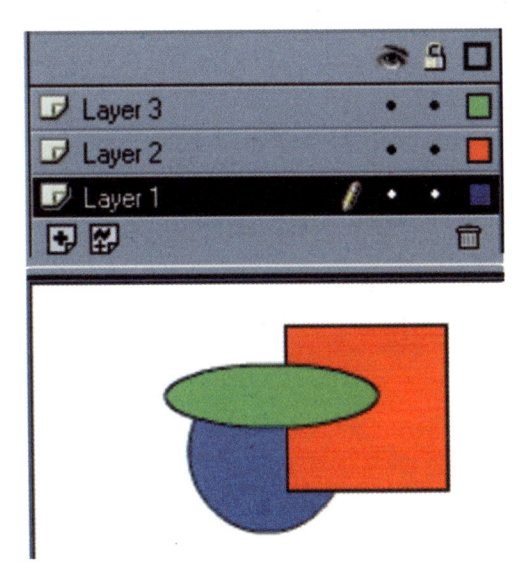

Figure 6.7 Three objects are stacked in the order of their respective layers

If we now grab the individual layers and drag them into a new order, as shown in Figure 6.8, you will see that the stacking order of the objects changes accordingly.

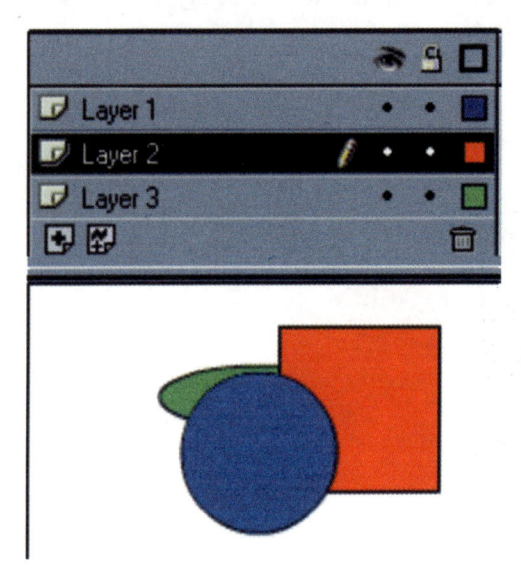

Figure 6.8 Reverse the layer order, and the stacking changes too

Although only one layer may be selected at any time, this does not mean you cannot edit items on other layers. For instance, if you were to have a stage set up as shown in Figure 6.8, you could select the paint bucket tool and click on each of the shapes in turn – without having to select and deselect layers – in order to fill each shape with a new colour.

Guide layers

We've already identified the two types of guide layers:

- plain guide layers;
- motion guide layers.

We will return to motion guides in Chapter 8; to create a plain guide layer, however, you have to convert an existing layer into a plain guide layer. (You will remember that we can convert a layer in this way by going to the Layer Properties dialog box and clicking on the appropriate radio button.)

There are many things you might wish to do with guide layers. For instance, you could place any objects on a guide layer to act as reference points when placing objects on other layers. These objects are not included in the final movie, however; they merely act as guides.

One particularly good use for guide layers is to place guidelines on them, similar to the guidelines used by page-layout programs such as Quark Xpress. By using the **snap to objects** feature (turned on from your **View** menu) you can then line up individual items to the guidelines in your guide layer.

Mask layers

A mask layer allows you to hide elements selectively in other layers that are linked to it – that is, elements in *masked* layers. You can think of a mask layer as an opaque sheet which has holes cut in it to allow you to see exactly what is underneath those holes, but no more.

*You can also create a guide layer by right-clicking the layer you want to define as a guide and choosing **Guide** from the pop-up menu.*

It's a good idea to lock guide layers once you have set them up so that you don't accidentally move the guides as you work with other layers.

Although it is possible to create an animated mask so that the window 'moves' over the masked layer, we'll stick for the moment with a static mask. (We'll cover animated masks in Chapter 8.)

There is no such thing as a semi-transparent hole; so too can a mask either be applied or not. There is no such thing as a semi-transparent mask. What this means in practice is that anything you put down on your mask layer will allow whatever is on the masked layer to show through. Any areas of the mask layer left untouched will block out what is contained underneath on the masked layer.

To show this in practice, consider Figure 6.9. Here we have created two plain layers. A rectangle is drawn on Layer 1 and an oval on Layer 2. We have filled the oval with a gradient running from black to green.

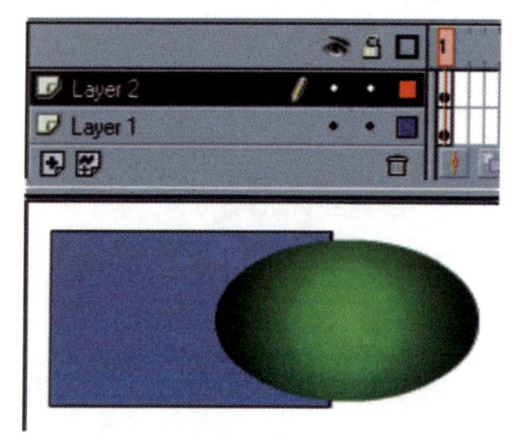

Figure 6.9 Two plain layers containing a rectangle and oval respectively

If we now convert Layer 2 into a mask layer (**right-click** on the name 'Layer 2' and select **mask**) and Layer 1 into its masked layer (in this case as there are only two layers, Layer 1 automatically becomes the masked layer), you will see in Figure 6.10 that the area of the rectangle overlapped by the oval is visible, while the remainder of the rectangle is hidden.

Notice, too, that the amount of shading within the oval makes no difference to the amount of rectangle that is visible.

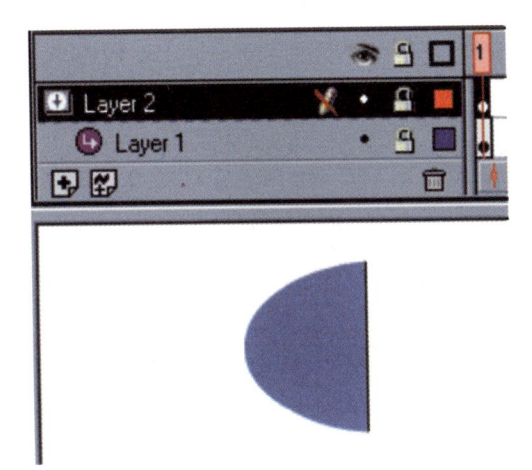

Figure 6.10 Layer 2 is now a mask layer with Layer 1 becoming its masked layer

If you want to make more than one masked layer attributable to one mask layer, you have to go to the Layer Properties dialog box (**Modify:Layer**) and then click on the radio button marked *Masked*, having first positioned the layer immediately below the mask layer.

In Figure 6.11 you can see that the mask layer is shown with a downward pointing arrow as its icon, while the masked layers each have a bent arrow icon and are indented below the mask layer.

A quick and easy way to create extra masked layers is to drag existing layers directly underneath the mask layer, or to select one of the masked layers and create a new layer by clicking on the + icon in the bottom left-hand corner of the Timeline.

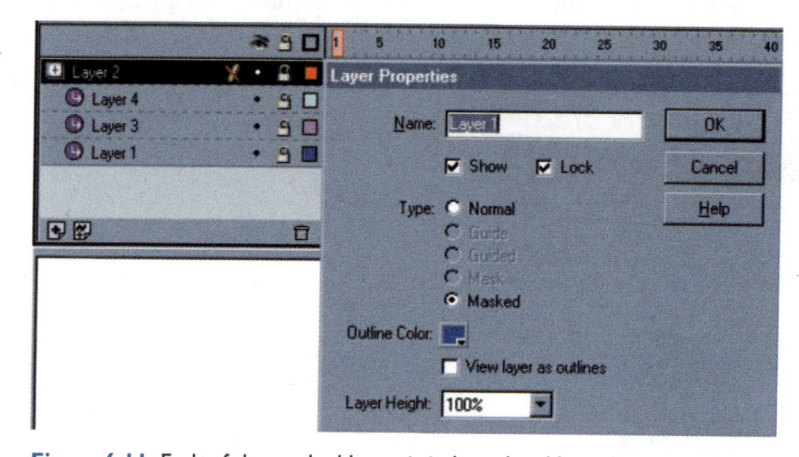

Figure 6.11 Each of the masked layers is indented and has a bent-arrow icon

When you create a mask layer with its masked sublayer you may not see anything different at first. This is because, for the masking to work, you have to lock the mask layer and *all* masked layers beneath before masking takes effect.

Paste in place

We saw in the last chapter how Flash allows you to paste objects from the Clipboard that have either been copied or cut from elsewhere within the Flash environment, or have been imported from another program.

Sometimes it is useful to copy or cut objects from different layers and paste them into another layer. Obviously it would be important to ensure that these objects are positioned exactly as they were in their original layers.

This is where **Paste in place** comes in useful. If you copied (or cut) an object and simply pasted it into a new layer, Flash would always paste it in the centre of the stage, ready for you to move and reposition.

However, if you go to the **Edit** menu and select **Paste in place**, the exact positioning from the original layer will be replicated in this new layer.

A shortcut for Paste in place is to use the combination of <Ctrl> <Shift> V.

Symbols and instances

7

Accessing libraries, symbols and instances
Creating symbols from graphic objects
Creating symbols without conversion
Symbols vs objects
Changing an instance ... in an instant
Swapping one instance for another
Breaking the link between instance and symbol

So far we've concentrated on the creation and manipulation of static objects. However, in a short while we will start to experiment with animations, and for that we will want to use copies of our objects over and over again as we place them in different parts of the scene, or use them in different movies.

Accessing libraries, symbols and instances

Objects are stored in *libraries*, when they are then referred to as *symbols*. Each copy of the symbol used in your animation or movie is then referred to as an *instance*.

To access the library of the movie that you are working on, you need to go to your **Window** menu and select **Library**. You can also get there by keying **<Ctrl> L** (Figure 7.1).

It is also possible to access symbols in libraries that you created for other movies. In this case you need to open up that particular library, which you do by going to the **File** menu and selecting **Open as Library** (or keying **<Ctrl> <Shift> O** Figure 7.2).

Flash not only keeps a library with each and every movie you create, it also has a collection of libraries, which it stores with its program files. When you installed Flash you will have created six libraries that you can access via the **Window:Common Libraries** menu (Figure 7.3). They are:

- Buttons
- Graphics
- Learning Interactions

When you go to the library of another movie you will not be allowed to modify its contents. Only the current library can be modified, although you are allowed to copy symbols within another library to your current library.

7: Symbols and instances

- Movie Clips
- Smart Clips
- Sounds.

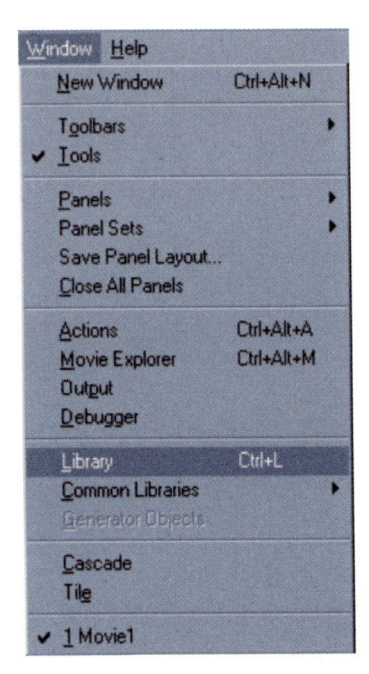

Figure 7.1 Access to the library of the current movie

Flash 5 for Windows

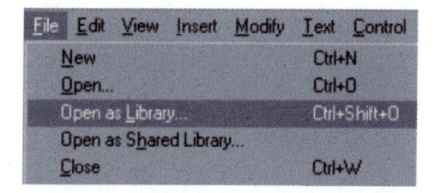

Figure 7.2 Getting to the symbols in another movie library

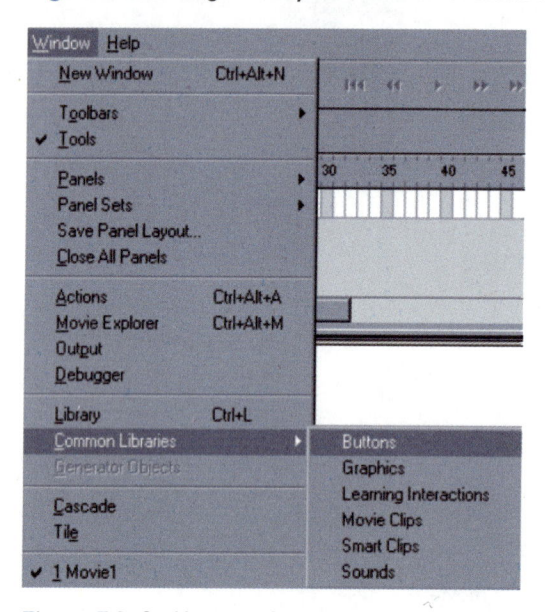

Figure 7.3 Six libraries of symbols are loaded by default with Flash 5

The Libraries directory
If you were to go to your *program files* directory and look 'inside' Flash 5 you would see a directory named *Libraries*. It contains matching files of the default libraries and each is a Flash file in its own right. (The extra folder contains SWF files for embedding within the Learning Interactions movie.) If you want to add default libraries to this menu you therefore only have to copy your Flash '.fla' files to the directory (Figure 7.4).

Libraries

- Learning Interactions UIs
- Buttons.fla
- Graphics.fla
- Learning Interactions.fla
- Movie Clips.fla
- Smart Clips.fla
- Sounds.fla

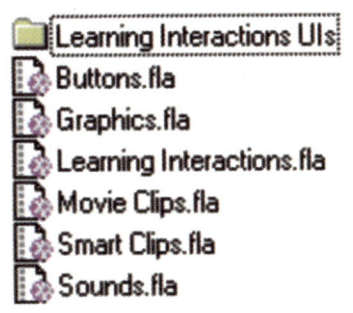

Figure 7.4 The Libraries directory within Flash's program files contains default library information

You might find it worthwhile to create a special collection of symbols that you use repeatedly in your projects – simply copy them from existing movies into a special file just for this purpose.

The Library window

When you open up a library you can view its contents in different ways and organise its contents the way it suits you – with hierarchical folders, for instance.

Flash offers information on when the symbol was last modified, how many times it has been used and what type of item it is, as well as any linkages to outside graphics programs that you may have set (Figure 7.5). You can expand and contract the window by clicking on the two respective icons at the top of the right-hand side slider bar. In expanded mode you can view the date that the symbol was last modified, and also count how many times it has been used. In the contracted mode you just get to see a list of the symbols in the library.

You will also see in Figure 7.6 that the Options menu enables you to create folders within a particular library. In Figure 7.5, for instance, we could have created a folder called *animals* into which we could have moved some of the symbols. To add symbols to a particular folder, all you need do is drag the symbol onto the folder icon to create a hierarchy – which will prove to be especially useful when you have a library with many symbols in it.

You can also see in Figure 7.5 that there are four icons in the bottom left-hand corner. These are, respectively:

1. New symbol
2. New folder
3. Symbol Properties
4. Delete item.

We'll return to items 1 and 3 in a moment. Item 2 – create new folder – is essentially the same as the *New Folder* option shown in Figure 7.6, while *Delete*

7: Symbols and instances

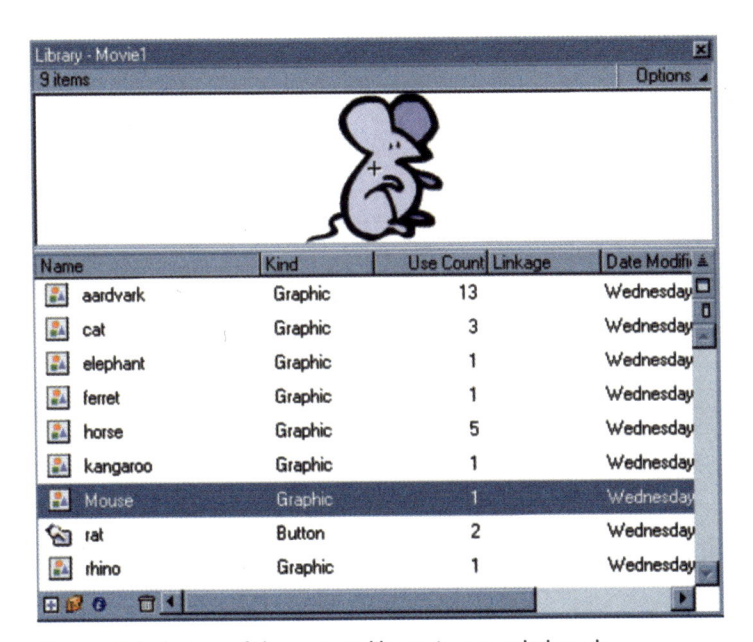

Figure 7.5 A view of the current library in expanded mode

*By default, the Use Counter does not automatically update, as it might slow down the program. However, if you go to the **Options** button (shown in the top right-hand corner of Figure 7.5) you can elect either to keep the Use Counts automatically updated or to be updated on demand (Figure 7.6).*

item (also accessible from the Options menu) allows you to delete a selected library item, although a confirmation box appears to check that you really do wish to delete the symbol since this action cannot be reversed. You can expand or close each library folder by double-clicking on it. This allows you more screen space to view the contents of other library folders.

Flash 5 for Windows

*Remember that if you delete a symbol from your library, it will also be deleted from your movie; so if you are at all in doubt, check the **Use Count** before you delete any symbols.*

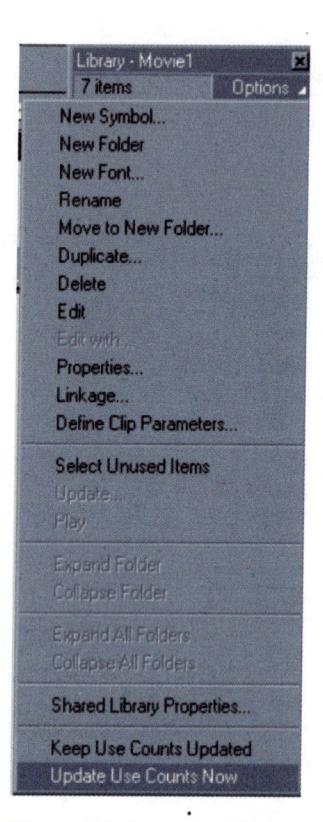

Figure 7.6 From the Library Options menu you can update Use Counts when you want to

Creating symbols from graphic objects

There will be occasions when you will wish to reuse a graphic object that you have either made or imported into Flash. By converting the graphic into a symbol you will best be able to reuse it without affecting the original in any way.

With the static object selected on your Stage, go to the **Insert** menu and select **Convert to Symbol** (or you can press **F8**). The Symbol Properties dialog box will appear (Figure 7.7) which allows you to choose whether you are creating a symbol of a graphic, a button or a movie clip. It also gives it a default name based on the number of symbols already in the library, but it is usually best if you give it a name that is meaningful so that you can locate the symbol easily at a later time.

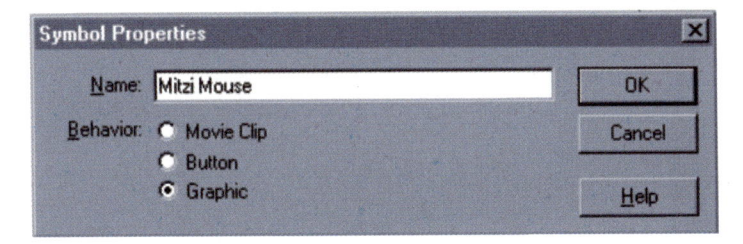

Figure 7.7 The Symbol Properties dialog box

Once you have clicked **OK** the object on the Stage becomes an *Instance* of the new symbol you have created.

You are no longer able to edit the graphic object directly on your Stage once you have converted it into a symbol. Instead you have to enter symbol editing mode (see below) to do so.

Creating symbols without conversion

If you wish to create a symbol that is to be used many times, it is not necessary to create a graphic first and then convert it to a symbol. Instead, you can create a symbol from scratch directly in **symbol editing** mode. Click on **New Symbol** in either the menu (Figure 7.6) or on its icon (Figure 7.5) to produce a new blank symbol.

The symbol editing entry button can be found at the top right-hand corner of the Stage (Figure 7.8) and this will bring up a drop-down list of available symbols, including your new blank symbol, which you can now select for editing.

Figure 7.8 Enter Symbol Editing mode via the click button at the top right-hand corner of the Stage

You'll know you're in symbol editing mode rather than working on the Stage because in the top left corner of the stage area is another pair of buttons, similar to those in Figure 7.9, which show the current editing status.

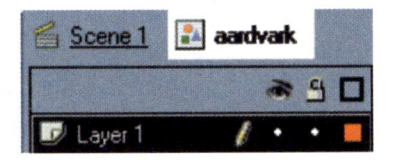

Figure 7.9 You can return to the normal stage editing mode by clicking on the left button tag

Symbols vs objects

At this point you might well be wondering why one should go to all the bother of using symbols when it is perfectly possible to reuse objects simply by copying them to another part of the Stage.

Well, of course you can work in that way if you want to; but by converting objects to symbols Flash only has to store the set of vector instructions for that object once. By then using multiple instances of that one symbol, Flash does not need to redefine the vector parameters each time the symbol is used. Instead it looks up its library of symbols and gleans the information from there.

You can then modify the different instances of each symbol – say, rotating it, colouring it, or whatever. But the basic set of instructions remains unaltered, and it is this that allows Flash to save a great deal of information in a nicely compact file.

You could, if you wished, skip the preview stage and simply drag the symbol name to the stage.

So, to place an instance of a symbol onto your Stage:

1. Select the layer on which you wish to place the instance.
2. Open the library containing the symbol whose instance you want to import.
3. Click once on the symbol to preview it in the upper library window (Figure 7.5).
4. Drag the preview to the stage where you want to place your instance.
5. Release the mouse.

Changing an instance ... in an instant

We have just mentioned that it is possible to change the appearance of an instance without altering the original symbol. In particular we can:

1. Scale it
2. Rotate it
3. Change its colour
4. Change its transparency.

Scaling and rotation are carried out in exactly the same way as you would scale or rotate any other object (see page 50), but you alter the colour and transparency by calling up the Instance Panel dialog box. Right-click on the instance to open the Effect Panel and then click on the drop-down menu. You are offered a choice of the following:

- Brightness
- Tint
- Alpha
- Advanced.

If we decided to alter the brightness of one of a pair of instances, for example, we would select the **Brightness** entry from the drop-down menu (Figure 7.10). The amount of brightness can be altered either by tweaking the slider tab or by entering an amount directly into the brightness value box.

Figure 7.10 Altering different instances of the same symbol

Similarly, we can change the colour balance by selecting **Tint** from the drop-down menu. Here we can not only choose the colour we want – either by keying in values to the RGB boxes, or by clicking on the colour grid – but also set the degree of tinting to be applied to the instance – again, by using either the slider control or by entering an exact amount (Figure 7.11).

If we want to alter the transparency of the instance we change its **Alpha** setting. A 100% setting makes it completely opaque; a 0% setting makes it transparent. Once again we can use either the slider or enter a number directly into the Alpha box (Figure 7.12).

Flash 5 for Windows

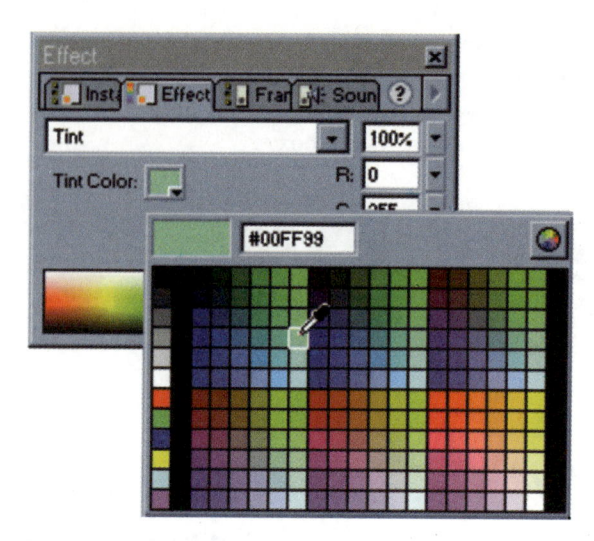

Figure 7.11 Changing an instance's colour settings

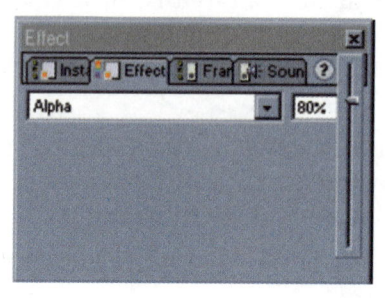

Figure 7.12 Setting the Alpha channel to 80% makes the instance partially opaque

Flash 5 also allows you to change a symbol instance's colour and transparency simultaneously. For this, you need to select **Advanced** from that drop-down menu. In Figure 7.13 you can see that each of the colour and alpha channels has two sliders. This may cause some confusion at first. Basically, the left and right sliders have different jobs to do. The *left* sliders cause changes in the values of the original colour balance while the *right* sliders add colour or opacity to the entire object.

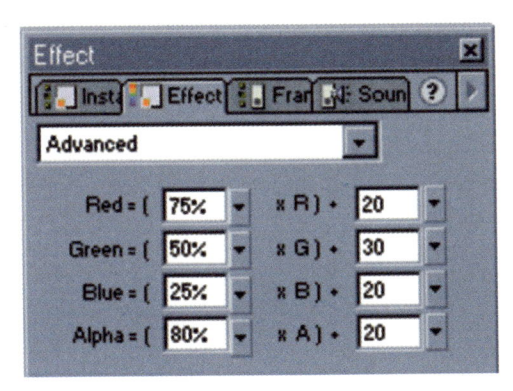

Figure 7.13 The special settings allow you to alter transparency together with the colour balance

Imagine, for instance, that you have three circles within your instance. One is coloured pure red (ie it has an RGB value of 255,0,0), another is pure green, while the third is pure blue.

If you reduce the value of the left-hand menu, it will reduce the amount of blue in the blue circle but will have no effect on the green or red circles since they have no blue element within them. However, if you increase the right-hand blue element, it adds blue to everything, including both the red and green circles, and these will now start to change colour. As usual, a little experimentation will soon make this clear.

Swapping one instance for another

Sometimes you might want to swap one instance for another **after** you have made changes to its size, rotation, colour, or whatever. Flash 5 makes this easy. Having made any modifications to the original instance, open up the **Instance Panel** dialog box (Figure 7.14).

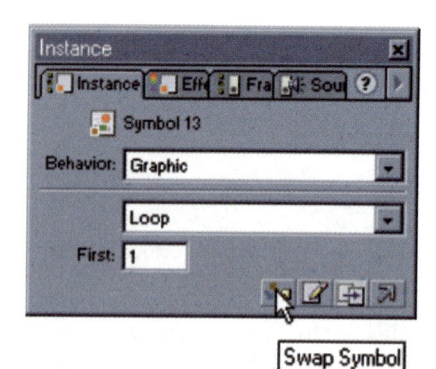

Figure 7.14 Using the Switch option in the definition section of the Properties dialog box

7: Symbols and instances

Now click on the **Swap Symbol** button to open up the Swap Symbol dialog box, choose an alternative symbol and click **OK** (Figure 7.15).

Remember that when you edit a symbol, rather than an instance, it will not only change the symbol that resides in your library but also every instance of the symbol within your movie.

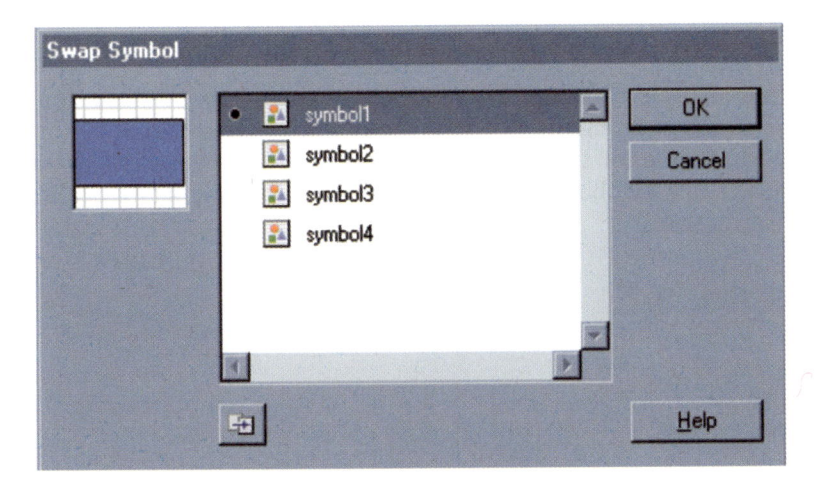

Figure 7.15 This is where you swap one symbol for another

If instead of swapping one instance with another you wish to edit a symbol, you can use the **Edit Symbol** button to the right of the Swap Symbol button we just used.

Breaking the link between instance and symbol

Finally, there may be occasions when you want to break the link between an instance of a particular symbol and the symbol itself. For example, you might wish to change the shape of a symbol in certain instances but not in others.

The best way to do this is to select the instance of the symbol whose link you want to break. Then from the **Modify** menu select **Break Apart** (or **<Ctrl> B**). You can then alter the shape (or whatever) of this object and even save it once more as a new symbol if you are likely to need this new shape again.

Animation 8

Animation basics
Frame types
Making a simple animation
Editing multiple frames
Setting the frame rate
Tweening animation
Moving objects along a predefined path
Shape tweening
Reversing frames
Animated masks
Saving your animations
A note about scenes

Animation basics

For obvious reasons, we have so far taken up more than half this book looking at the basics of using Flash. However, it is only when we move on to the use of animations that Flash really comes into its own. It is, after all, the main reason that you probably bought the software in the first place.

In Flash you can:

- move an object across the Stage;
- increase or decrease its size;
- rotate the object;
- change its colour;
- change its basic shape;
- make it fade in or fade out.

There are two basic methods one can use in creating a Flash animation:

1. Make frames individually.
2. Create starting and ending frames and let Flash '**tween**' between them.

Frame types

If you look at the Timeline you will see that there are very many cells or **frames** within your movie. Assuming you have a totally blank Flash Stage, you will see that all the frames look blank (Figure 8.1).

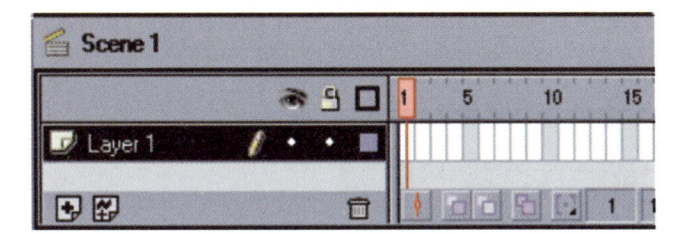

Figure 8.1 At the start of a new movie, all the frames in the Timeline look blank

*An even faster way of creating a keyframe is to use your **F6** function key.*

Whenever you place an object within the Timeline of a movie, you have to create a **keyframe**. Normally you would leave some of the frames blank between the first keyframe and the next – we'll see why in a moment. Let's insert a keyframe into frame 5. Click once on frame 5 and then use the **Insert** menu (or **right-click** on it) to turn it into a keyframe (the latter is much quicker and easier!). Straight away, the frame divisions before frame 5 disappear, and a vertical line is placed before the keyframe (Figure 8.2).

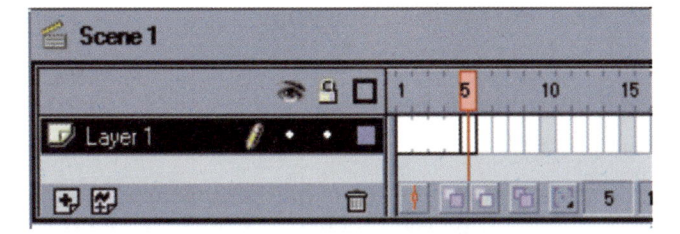

Figure 8.2 Inserting a keyframe at frame 5 places a vertical line in front of it

Let's now place an object – say, a circle – onto the Stage at this frame. Straight away a bullet is placed into the keyframe to show it is no longer empty (Figure 8.3).

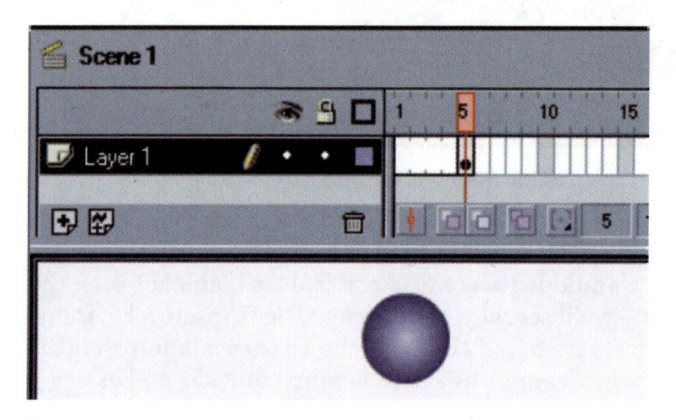

Figure 8.3 A blob in a keyframe shows it is no longer empty

Next, let's insert a blank keyframe into frame 10. You can:

- right-click on the frame and select **blank keyframe**;
- go to your **Insert** menu and select **blank keyframe**;
- click once on the frame and press **F7**.

You'll notice that the Stage area is blank. The circle has disappeared. You'll also see that a small vertical rectangle is placed just before frame 10, and that the frames between 5 and 10 have turned grey (Figure 8.4). In addition, if you place your cursor over any of these greyed-out frames it will change into a hand shape. (Placing the cursor over a white frame reverts it to a normal pointer – Figure 8.5.)

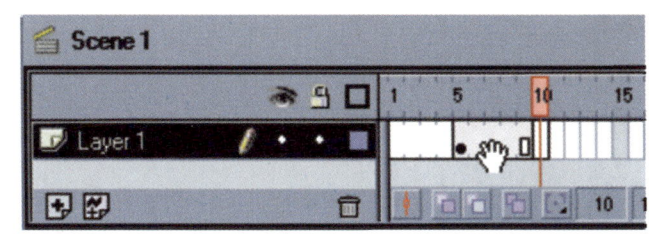

Figure 8.4 Inserting a blank keyframe adds a small rectangle just before it

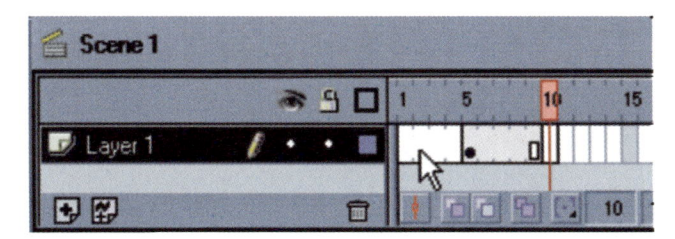

Figure 8.5 The cursor changes back to normal when it isn't over a keyframe or its associated frames

If we click on any frame between 5 and 10 – ie in the greyed-out frames – we will continue to see the circle on the Stage Area (Figure 8.6). In effect, the blank frame has deleted everything from sight from frame 10 onwards.

*You can alter the size with which you view the Timeline in order to see more or fewer frames. Go to the **Frame View** pop-up menu to the top right of the Stage and select an option (Figure 8.7).*

*Although Flash talks about 'Inserting' keyframes, it actually does nothing of the sort! What it really does is to convert an existing frame into a keyframe. The number of frames remains constant. If instead you use the **insert frame** command, then Flash does indeed add extra frames.*

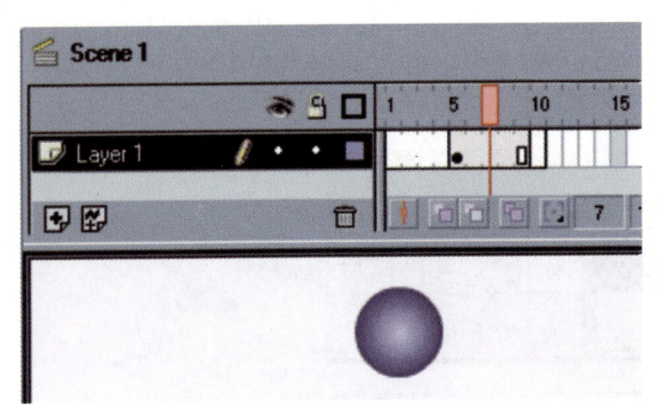

Figure 8.6 We have placed a filled circle in frame 5 (note the solid bullet) so clicking on frame 7 will continue to show the circle

So far we have had the option of adding either:

1. a blank keyframe
2. a keyframe.

If you wish to change the contents of the scene completely, go for option 1. If you intend solely to make minor changes, plump for option 2. The latter duplicates whatever has gone before, allowing you to add objects, move things around, or whatever.

You may quite often find the need to insert extra frames, and a quick way to do this, apart from laboriously inserting single frames, is to copy and paste empty

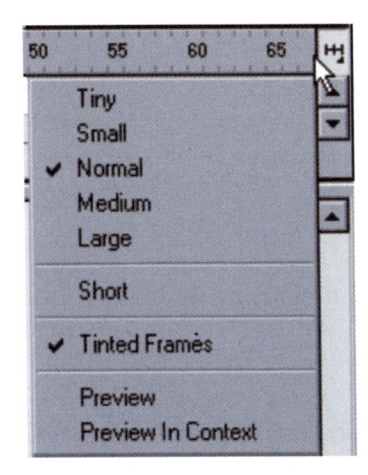

Figure 8.7 Select your Timeline size from the Frame View pop-up menu

frames from the end of the Timeline into the point in the Timeline you wish to expand. However, you cannot simply copy and paste using the normal Windows shortcuts, otherwise you will paste over the frames already in existence. Instead, **right-click** on your selected number of empty frames and select **Copy Frames** or **Paste Frames** as appropriate.

Just as there are two commands for inserting frames – depending on whether you really do wish to add an extra frame rather than a keyframe – so, too, are there two commands (confusingly contained in the **Insert** menu!) for removing frames:

*You can also copy and paste frames by using the keyboard with **<Ctrl> <Alt> C** or **<Ctrl> <Alt> V** as appropriate.*

Sometimes, when you try to delete a keyframe, it appears that Flash refuses to carry out your instructions. This is most likely to happen if you try to delete a keyframe without deleting the contents of the in-between frames that have picked up their information from the keyframe you are trying to delete. In its attempt to make sense of your conflicting instructions, Flash creates a virtual keyframe. The result is that you end up trying to delete a keyframe, which Flash replaces with an identical one! Instead, select all the associated in-between frames with your keyframe and delete the lot in one go.

1. Clear keyframe
2. Delete frame.

The former simply removes the keyframe status from your selected frame – it does not remove it from the Timeline. The latter, on the other hand, deletes the frame entirely from your movie and reduces the number of frames accordingly.

Making a simple animation

Let's kick off by creating an extremely simple animation using frame-by-frame animation. Open up a new Flash document and switch on the grid (**View:Grid:Show Grid**) for ease of accurate placing. Select the first frame and on your Stage draw a circle.

Next, click on the second frame and insert a keyframe as described above. Straight away two things happen: a bullet is added to show that frame 2 is now a keyframe, and the circle you drew before becomes selected. Drag the selected circle to a new position a few centimetres to the right. Repeat once more with the third frame (Figure 8.8).

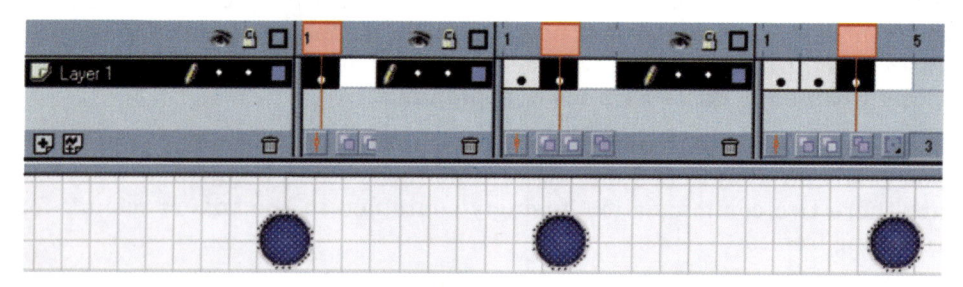

Figure 8.8 Using insert keyframe commands to duplicate and move the circle

If you now click frames 1, 2 and 3 in turn you will see the circle 'move' to its new positions. However, to see your movie automatically, go to your **Control** menu and select **Play**. It's all over pretty quickly, but if instead you go to **Control:Loop Playback** and then **Play** the scene again it will continue looping through your movie.

You can step through the frames sequentially by clicking on the '<' or '>' keys repeatedly.

Smoothing your animation

If you want to smooth the jerky animation you just created it is necessary to insert more keyframes into the animation and reposition the circle with smaller movements. It means that the final file size will be greater, of course, but you need to strike a happy balance between smoother motion and keeping the file size to a minimum.

Between frames 1 and 2, and frames 2 and 3, insert frames from the **Insert** menu and nudge the circle along for each extra frame. Now when you preview your movie the action should be smoother, but it will probably still appear jerky. What can we do next?

Well, maybe part of the problem lies in the fact that the circle is not moving equidistantly between each keyframe. To help with the accurate placing of each circle let's use Flash's **Onion skinning** facility – turn this on by clicking on the button shown in Figure 8.9. Now you can see the contents of each keyframe at once. However, you cannot edit the dimmed circles except by selecting their individual keyframes, when that particular dimmed circle will become full-colour.

If you are not able to see as many onion skins as you were expecting, click on the **Modify Onion Markers** button (Figure 8.10) and select the option of viewing more frames. Alternatively, drag the onion skin markers shown as brackets around your keyframes at the top of the Timeline (Figure 8.11).

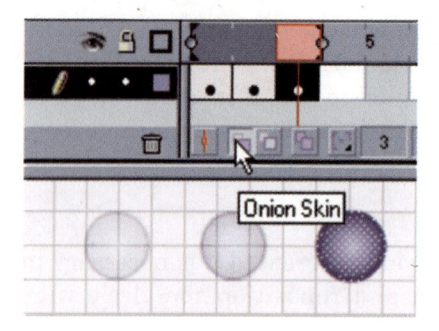

Figure 8.9 Turning on the Onion Skin feature allows you to see all keyframes at once

If you click on the button to the immediate right of the onion skin button the dimmed objects will become outlines only, allowing you to judge placing overlapping objects more easily.

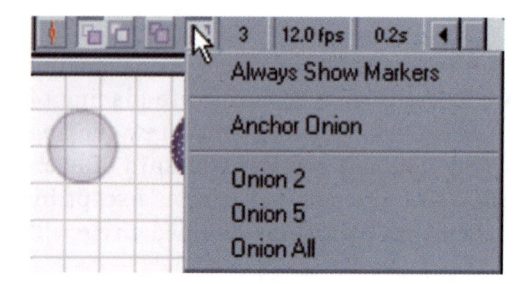

Figure 8.10 Adjusting the Onion Skin view

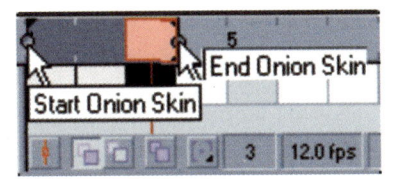

Figure 8.11 You can drag the Onion Skin outer markers to view more or fewer skins

Editing multiple frames

It may well be that, having created your animation frames, you want to reposition one of your animated objects. You could, in theory, move each individual instance of your object and realign them using the grid. A much better option is to use the **Edit Multiple Frames** option that you can switch on by using the button to the right of the Onion Skin button (Figure 8.12). By turning on this option you can effectively edit objects in different keyframes simultaneously.

Having clicked this button, select the arrow tool in the toolbar and drag a rectangle around all the instances of the circle on your Stage. Each of the circles is selected. Now go to the **Window** menu and use **Panels:Align** to get each of the circles lined up with one another.

Setting the frame rate

Flash allows you to set the frame rate which determines how many frames are displayed every second. Set the frame rate too fast, and the movie will rush past in a blur. Too slow, and the animation will be jerky. Normally, the standard rate for a feature film is 24 frames per second (fps). On the web, 12 fps is a good rate. By default, Flash sets the frame rate at 12 fps.

Once you choose the Edit Multiple Frames option, onion skinning no longer works, since you have effectively chosen to edit each keyframe instance at once.

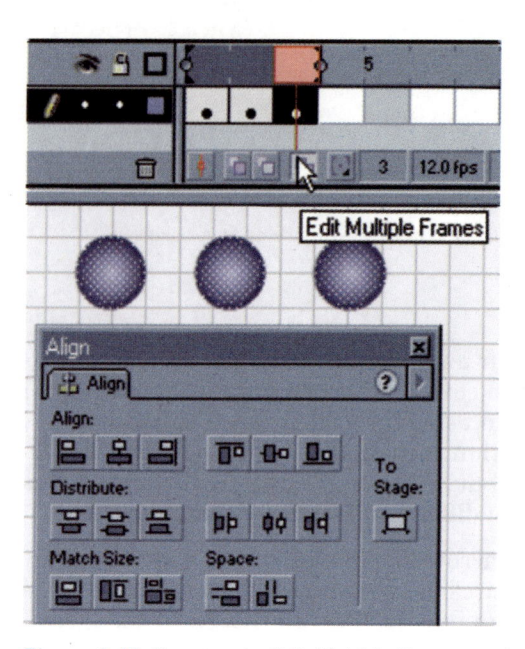

Figure 8.12 By using the Edit Multiple Frames option you can align and space each of the object instances

To change the default setting, which affects the entire movie, go to the **Modify** menu and select **Movie**. Alternatively you can double-click the frame rate value at the bottom of the Timeline. The **Movie Properties** dialog box appears (Figure 8.13).

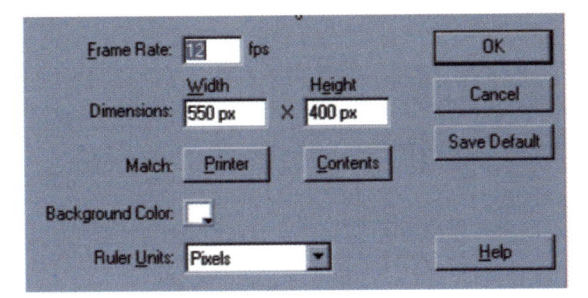

Figure 8.13 Setting the frame rate in the Movie Properties dialog box

Although the frame rate of a movie remains constant, you can speed up or slow down a particular section of a movie by adding or deleting frames from that section. Inserting in-between frames adds very little to the overall file size, but if you add keyframes to show the object in a slightly different position each time, the overall movie file will increase in size considerably.

We saw in Figure 8.7 that it is possible to increase the size of the frame representations within the Timeline. From that same drop-down menu you can also select either **Preview** or **Preview in Context**, which will give you previews of your individual frames either at full size or in relation to one another (Figure 8.14).

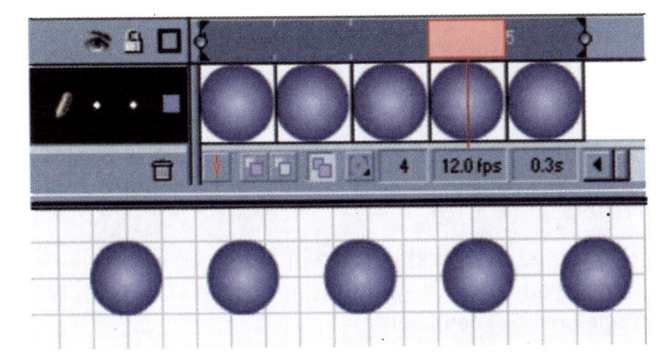

Figure 8.14 'Preview' your frames – if you have a large enough screen!

The word 'tweening' is derived from the action of creating in-between frames, which is what cartoon animators used to do laboriously by hand when creating cartoon feature films.

Tweening animation

Frame-by-frame animation has two major drawbacks associated with it: it is extremely time consuming, and it also creates very large files. By using **Tweening**, Flash gets round both these problems.

Tweening comes in two forms:

1. Motion tweening.
2. Shape tweening.

By defining the beginning and end keyframes, Flash creates a series of frames with incremental changes that change the first keyframe to the last keyframe, morphing from one to the other.

Motion tweening

Let's create a simple motion tween to move a circle from the left of our stage to the right. First, create a movie and, in keyframe 1, add a circle to the Stage (Figure 8.15).

With frame 1 still selected, select **Create Motion Tween** from the **Insert** menu. The circle is made into a symbol, which Flash calls, by default, 'Tween 1'. Now select frame 10 and **Insert:Frame**. A dotted line appears in the Timeline showing there is an unresolved tween operation. Convert frame 10 to a keyframe, however, and the tween information thinks it is complete. The dotted line turns into an arrow (Figure 8.15).

However, so far nothing has changed. Select the circle in frame 10 and move it to a new position and now, when you **Play** the animation (or press **Enter**), the circle moves smoothly from one side to the other.

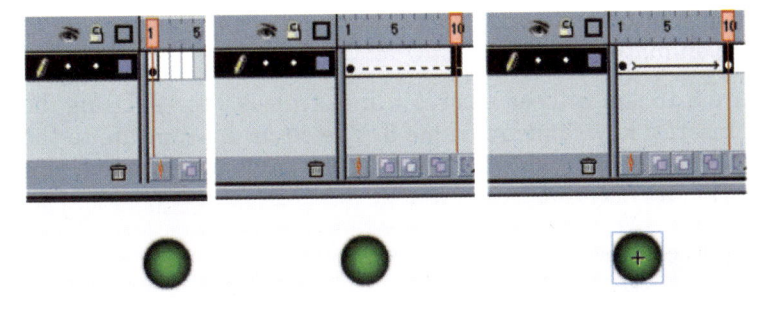

Figure 8.15 Creating a motion tween

You can view the tweening that has been created by looking at the individual frames with the onion skinning turned on (Figure 8.16).

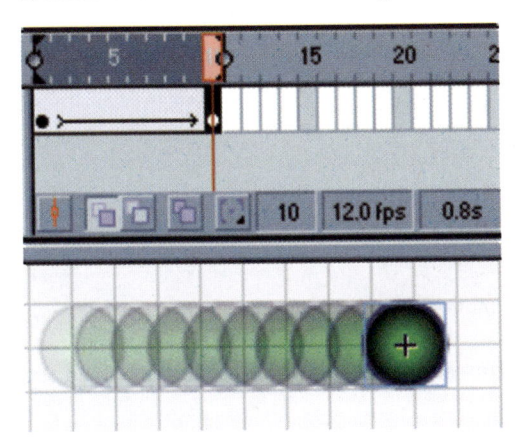

Figure 8.16 Viewing the motion tween with onion skins showing

You can add keyframes into an already-created motion tween, allowing you to alter the path of the animation if you want to.

If you look at Figure 8.16 you will see an arrow links frames 0 to 10. Using the right-click menu, insert a keyframe on frame 6. The circle appropriate to the tween position at frame 6 is highlighted. Now, drag the circle instance to a new position and let go (Figure 8.17).

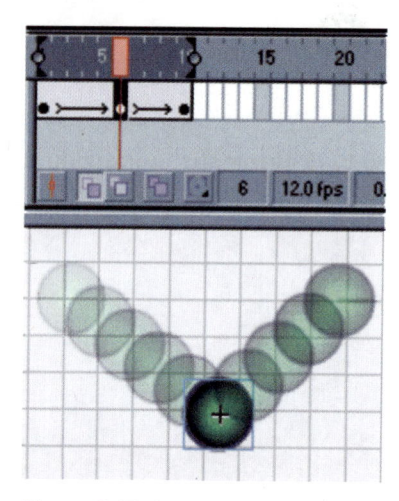

Figure 8.17 Inserting an extra keyframe into a motion tween

Now when you play your animation, the redefined path will be substituted for your original path.

Tweening colour changes and fading in and out

As well as using Motion Tween to move objects around the stage, you can use it to change the colours of objects, or even to fade an object in and out of the picture.

Let's start once again with a circle positioned in frame 1. You can only motion tween grouped objects or symbols, so we first convert this circle into a symbol by clicking on **Insert:Convert to Symbol**. In the Timeline we next create a keyframe at, say, frame 10. With keyframe 10 still selected, go to the **Modify** menu and select **Instance** and then click on the **Effect** tab. (Alternatively select **Window:Panel:Effect**). By selecting **Tint** in the drop-down menu we can select a new colour for our circle (Figure 8.18) and also how much (what percentage) of tint to apply to the object.

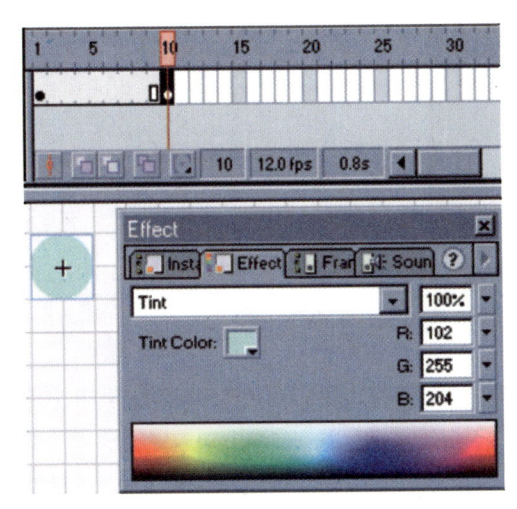

Figure 8.18 Changing the colour of the instance

Flash 5 for Windows

If, instead of changing colour, you wish to fade out the object, choose **Alpha** from the drop-down menu. The Alpha setting determines the transparency of your object. A zero value effectively washes your object completely from the picture.

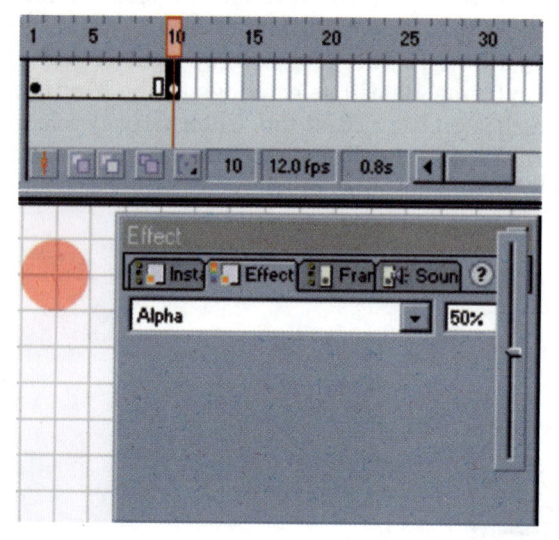

Figure 8.19 Changing the transparency of the instance with its Alpha channel

Finally, you can test your colour change by playing your animation in the normal way.

Tweening objects that change size

Not only can you create a motion tween that moves your object and changes colour, you can change its size as well (Figure 8.20). In your final keyframe resize the instance, but before you try out your animation, right-click on one of the frames and select **Panels:Frame**. Ensure that the ✓ box labelled **Scale** is selected.

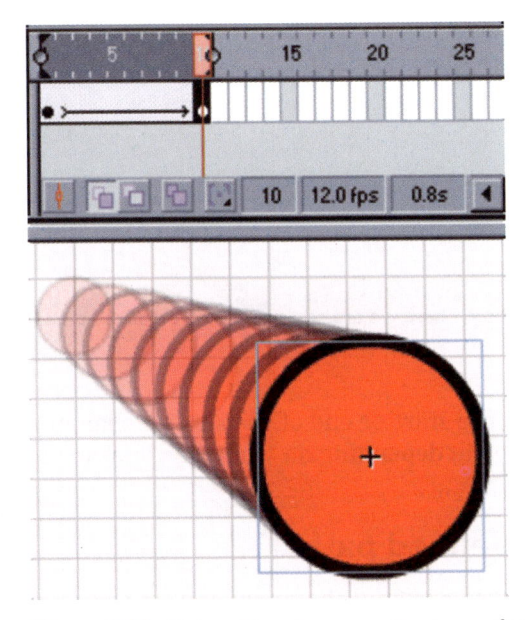

Figure 8.20 Onion skins show a motion tween for an object that changes size as it moves

Rotating objects

If you want to rotate an object as part of your motion tween, you need to give more information than just two keyframes can offer. If you think about it, an object could rotate clockwise or anticlockwise, or even flip over. Flash allows you to define the method of rotation by bringing up that same **Panel:Frame** we used just a moment ago (Figure 8.21).

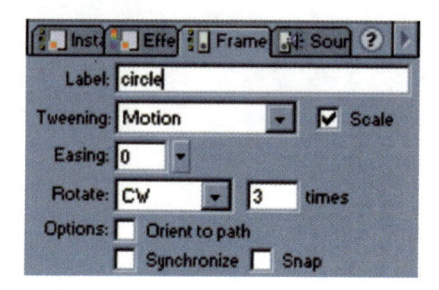

Figure 8.21 Determining the direction of rotation – here we are rotating the object three times clockwise

You can also slow down the rotation at the start or end of the spin by changing the value of the **Easing** slider up or down, depending on whether you want to 'ease in' or 'ease out'.

Moving objects along a predefined path

It's all very well being able to move objects around the Stage in a collection of straight lines, but in real life you will want to move the objects along curves and trajectories as well. This is where the use of motion guides comes into its own.

Motion guides define the paths for a tweened object to move along. Each guide has to be created on a separate layer, but you can use one guide to control a number of objects on different layers.

To create a motion guide layer, start off a new Flash document and place an object in the first frame. Convert it into a symbol (**Insert:Convert to Symbol**) and then create a straight line tween to, say, frame 20 as above.

At the bottom of the Timeline we next click the **Add Guide Layer** button (Figure 8.22), which adds a new layer directly above the layer you selected. The layer you were working on is now indented under the Guide layer.

Figure 8.22 We start by creating a straight line tween

Once you have selected this guide layer you can draw the path you want your object to follow by using the pencil tool, oval, rectangle, line or brush. In the Frame Panel dialog box, ensure the **Snap** check box is ticked and then tweak the start and end objects directly over the ends of the motion path you have

It's a good idea, once you have created your motion path, to lock this layer so that you cannot alter it accidentally.

just defined. Although the motion path is visible at the present time (Figure 8.23), it will not be shown in the final movie.

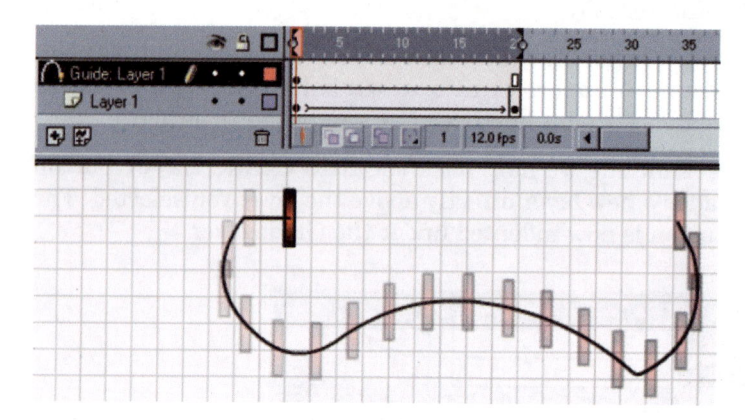

Figure 8.23 The object follows the defined motion path

In Figure 8.23 you can see that the object – although it slavishly follows the motion path – remains at its original angle. But in normal motion you would expect the object to twist and turn in sympathy with the direction of movement.

This time, therefore, ensure that the **Orient to path** check box shown in Figure 8.21 is checked. The object should now always face the direction of movement (Figure 8.24).

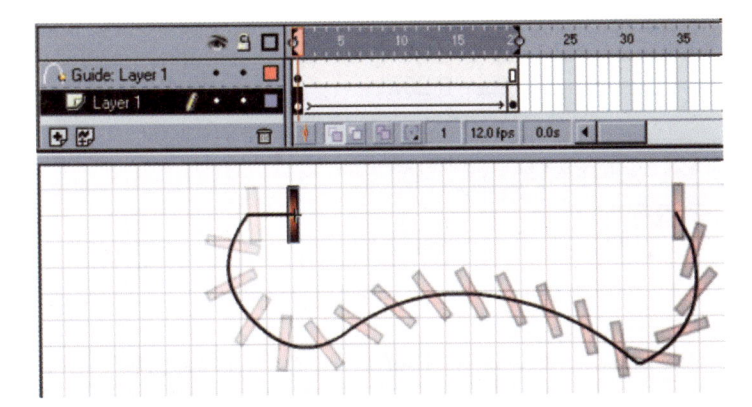

Figure 8.24 The object now rotates in the direction of movement

Shape tweening

Just as you can tween objects to make them move from one part of the Stage to another, so too can you get an object to morph into another. This type of tweening is called **shape tweening**.

Just as in motion tweening, shape tweening requires you to define the beginning and end shape; Flash then creates the in-between frames morphing one shape gradually into the next.

There are some functions that shape tweening can do that can also be carried out in motion tweening. The shape that you wish to tween might, for instance, be a different colour from your original shape. It follows, therefore, that shape

If you have sudden changes of direction in your motion guide, Flash may have difficulty aligning the object at every frame (see the bottom right-hand corner of figure 8.24, for instance). If your moving object looks as if it needs a bit of help, there is nothing to stop you inserting an extra keyframe or two and manually realigning the direction each instance faces.

It may seem obvious, when you think of it, but it is important to understand that whereas motion tweening works on groups and symbols, shape tweening requires the objects to be editable in order to work.

tweening can be instructed to change an object's colour as well as its size and location. You cannot, however, get Flash to rotate an object or move it along a motion guide using shape tweening (Figure 8.25).

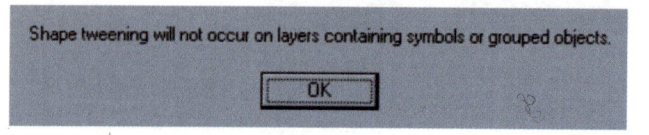

Figure 8.25 Flash warns you if you try to shape tween the wrong type of object

Let's start by transforming a circle into a square – an example of morphing simple lines and fills. We'll create a new Flash document and draw a circle in frame 1. For ease of demonstration we will make the circle in outline form only, although we could just as easily have made it filled.

Next we select frame 10 in the Timeline, but this time we'll **Insert** a **Blank Keyframe** which has the effect of removing everything from the stage at this particular frame. Now we can create a square on the stage. Don't worry about the exact placing of the square right now, we can deal with that later.

Now we'll open up the frame panel and select the **Tweening** menu. In the drop-down menu we select Shape tweening (Figure 8.26). The Blend type menu allows you to choose whether you want Flash to retain any sharp corners and straight lines as it transforms from one shape to another (**Angular**) or if you want it to smooth out the tweening shapes (**Distributive**). As before, the **Easing** value allows you to change the transition speed at either the start or end of the tween.

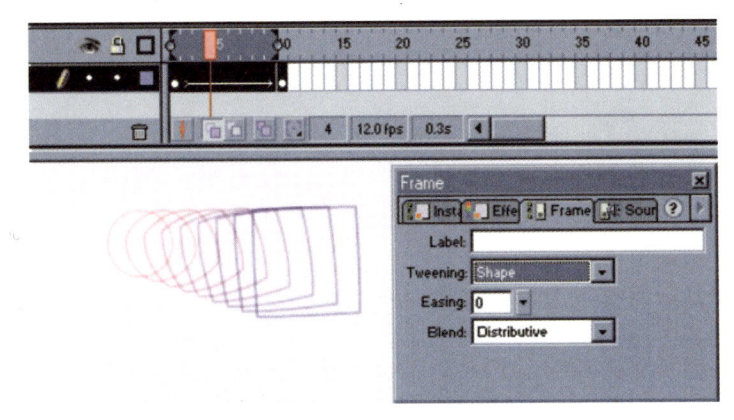

Figure 8.26 Selecting Shape Tweening in the Frame Properties dialog box

When we click **OK**, Flash morphs the circle into a square. On the Timeline, if we have Tinted Frames active (which is set in the pop-up menu at the end of the Timeline – Figure 8.7), then Flash turns the frames containing the shape tween light green (once we have switched off onion skinning, that is).

The onion skinning shows clearly that the circle and square are not nearly aligned. By choosing either frame 1 or frame 10 we can nudge the circle or square one on top of the other so that they are perfectly aligned (Figure 8.27).

Shape tweening multiple objects
Because Flash would have difficulty in determining which starting shape morphs to which ending shape if you had more than one object on a particular layer, it is advisable to restrict yourself to a single object on any layer you wish to shape tween.

Figure 8.27 At last the circle and square are perfectly aligned

This is best illustrated if we attempt to create the following morph. We'll place a square and circle on one layer and ask Flash to morph to the same square and circle, but placed in a different area of the Stage. As you can see from Figure 8.28, Flash has chosen to morph the square into the circle and vice versa in preference to crossing their morphing paths.

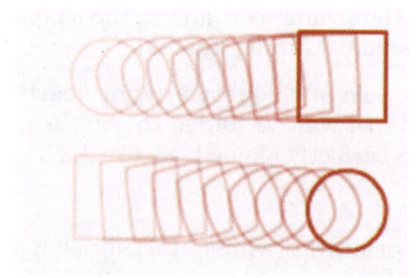

Figure 8.28 The circle and square have morphed into one another in perference to crossing over

Using Shape Hints to improve your morphing

When we transformed a circle into a square it was fairly obvious how Flash would morph the shape. Sometimes, however, especially with complicated shapes, Flash has difficulty interpreting exactly what you want it to do. You can help it by providing **Shape Hints**.

Say that you wanted to morph the fish in Figure 8.29 into a mouse. (We've actually used two images in Flash's library of symbols. As you cannot shape tween symbols or grouped objects, we had to break them apart first using the **Modify** menu.)

Figure 8.29 Preparing to morph a fish into a mouse

We begin by placing the fish in frame 1 and inserting a blank keyframe in frame 10 where the mouse is then placed. Bring up the frame panel dialog box and ask it to shape tween from one animal to the other.

Select frame 1 if it is not already selected and either go to your **Modify** menu and choose **Transform:Add Shape Hint** or – far quicker – key **<Ctrl> <Shift> H**. A little red spot appears in the centre of the fish image, which is exactly duplicated in the centre of the mouse image when you move across to frame 10. This red spot marks your first shape hint's position. Unlike the way in which some morphing programs work, it is important in Flash to place shape hints in order (either clockwise or anticlockwise) around the *edge* of the object. So drag the red spot, say, to the top of the fish's head and then, in frame 10, drag the red spot to the top of the mouse's head.

Continue to place shape hints around the edge of each animal (Figure 8.30) so that Flash is given help in determining which parts of the fish should morph to their respective mouse parts.

If you think you have made a mistake with the placing of your shape hints, you can reposition them at any time you want. Alternatively, you can remove a shape hint by clicking on the initial keyframe and then dragging the hint off the stage.

Figure 8.30 Six shape hints have been added to help with the morph

Getting shape tweens to move along a path

We've already said that you cannot use shape tweening to move an object along a guide path. So what do you do if you want a circle, say, to turn into a square, but to move along a loop as it does so?

The answer is to use a combination of shape tweening and motion tweening.

As we did before, create a shape tween to morph a circle into a square. Let's do it over 20 frames, so that the last keyframe is defined as frame 20. Now select all 20 frames in the tween sequence and, using the **Insert** menu, convert all 20 frames to keyframes.

Flash keeps the tween information within each keyframe that you have just created. As Flash allows you to place any keyframe object where you want, it is a simple matter to drag each instance to a position on the Stage. To get more accuracy, you could create a new guide layer and draw a curved line on it. Go to the **View:Guides** menu and select **Snap to Guides**. Now when you drag the object close to the guideline it should snap into place against the line.

Reversing frames

Sometimes a seemingly complex animation can be made much simpler by reversing a sequence of some of your frames. For instance, if an object grows and then shrinks, why not save yourself time and effort by creating the growth sector and then simply copying and reversing these frames for the second part of the animation.

Flash can do this very easily. In your Timeline, select the frames you want to copy by highlighting them and then selecting **Copy Frames** from the edit menu.

Now paste these frames into position immediately behind the frames you have created using the same menu. Your animation now contains two growth animations, one immediately following the other. Select the second set of frames that you have just pasted and from your **Modify** menu, select **Frames:Reverse**. Flash reverses the order of the second set of frames, creating the illusion of an object growing and then contracting.

Animated masks

We learned in Chapter 6 that you can selectively hide or reveal objects by using mask layers. There is no reason why that mask should not, itself, be a moving object. You can use any of the three types of tweening – motion tweening, shape tweening or frame-by-frame animation – to create a moving mask.

If we wanted some text to be revealed by a 'spotlight' over time, we could make a mask that contained a solid circle which was motion tweened across the Stage. Any text in the associated masked layer would then automatically be revealed as the circle moved over it.

The first thing, then, is to add some text somewhere on the Stage and then to fill the following frames by inserting a keyframe at, say, frame 20. Now create a mask layer and in frame 1 of this mask layer place a solid circle over the start of the text. Remember that you will need to unlock the mask layer in order to be able to edit it.

Next we create a motion tween along the mask layer such that the circle ends up at the right-hand end of the text at the end of the tween process (Figure 8.31).

Figure 8.31 We add some text to the Stage, add a mask layer and add a circle

If we turn on our onion skin view we can see that a series of circles runs along the text. Remember that any solid area in the mask layer allows us to see the layer below; any clear area in the mask hides the area below. The effect, when you run **Control:Test Movie**, is text that is sequentially highlighted by a moving circle. Very impressive output for very little work!

Saving your animations

So, we've created our tweened image and we could, if we wanted, simply save it along with the rest of the movie. However, we've already seen that if it is at all possible that the same sequence could be reused, it will take up much less memory if we save this moving sequence as a graphic symbol in its own right and then reuse the graphic symbol from our library.

Flash allows us to save moving images in one of two ways:

1. Animated graphic symbol.
2. Movie clip symbol.

*The only clue that a library symbol is actually an animated symbol is by looking in the top right-hand corner of the library window. An animated symbol has **Stop** and **Play** buttons showing, with which you can preview your animation.*

Animated symbols are unable to save any sound tracks or interactive features (both of which we'll be covering later). Movie clips, on the other hand, are self-contained and can be positioned in just one frame of your movie frames. If you are likely to want to edit an instance of your animation when it is reused, you should save it as an animated symbol.

To create an animated graphic symbol, highlight all the frames in all the layers you want to save and **Edit:Copy frames**. Next, create a symbol by selecting **Insert:New Symbol**. From the resulting properties dialog box choose **Graphic**.

Once you click on **OK**, a new symbol is created in the library, but it has just one frame and one timeline. In frame 1, **Edit:Paste Frames** to copy the animation frames into their own new symbol.

Remember when you come to use the animated symbol later on to allow enough frames to contain the entire symbol clip, unless, of course, you want to have overlapping Timelines to allow simultaneous actions.

To create a movie clip symbol, you do exactly the same as before when saving an animated symbol, except that you choose **Movie Clip** rather than **Graphic** in the symbol properties dialog box (Figure 8.32).

Figure 8.32 Creating a new movie clip

Movie clips have their own Timeline and will play continuously until such time as a new blank keyframe is placed within that timeline to stop the movie running. Unlike animated graphic symbols, movie clips need to be exported to a test mode before they can be viewed. This is simple enough, however. From your **Control** menu choose either **Test Movie** or **Test Scene** to get Flash to export the movie clip to a shockwave format (.swf) file which it will then display.

A note about scenes

Creating a movie with 10 or 20 frames is easy enough to handle, but what happens if your final movie runs to hundreds of frames? You could, in theory, scroll backwards and forwards along the Timeline finding the relevant bits of your movie. It's much easier, however, to break up the movie into manageable-sized chunks called **Scenes**.

You can create scenes and arrange the order in which they play by going to **Window:Panels:Scene** (Figure 8.33).

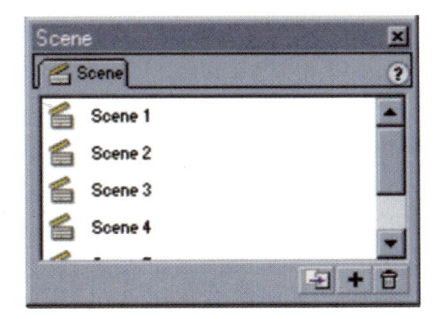

Figure 8.33 The Scene inspector window

Each scene title can be dragged one above the other to change the order in which they play. Once Flash has finished with one scene it automatically starts playing the next one. It follows, therefore, that in order to maintain continuity between scenes it is a good idea to copy the entire contents of each layer of the last frame of your current scene to the beginning frame of the next scene to ensure the accurate placing of any elements on the stage.

You can tell at a glance which scene you are editing by the flag that comes up to the left of the Timeline, as in Figure 8.34.

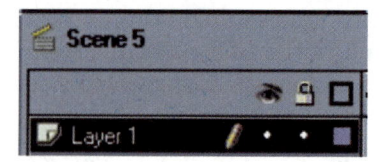

Figure 8.34 Flash leaves you in no doubt as to which scene you are editing

Scenes are particularly useful when using interactivity within your movie: 'If such an event happens then jump to scene 5; otherwise jump to scene 7' for instance.

We will be examining interactive movies in the next chapter. See you there!

Interactivity 9

Action types
Frame labels and comments
Some basic actions
Buttons
Interactivity with buttons
On (MouseEvent)s

You'll save yourself time and eyestrain if you assign action frames to one layer of your Timeline only. That way, when you are searching for an action frame in the middle of a long movie, it will be much easier to find it. Name the layer 'Actions' and lock it so that you cannot assign objects to it by accident.

So far we've been concentrating on sequential animation – where Flash moves from one scene to the next, for instance. However, there is no reason why you cannot instruct Flash to move from the end of one sequence to the start of another, or from any point in a scene to any other scene or frame you wish.

You give instructions to Flash by assigning actions to frames and buttons. A frame with an action assigned to it has an 'a' displayed within the Timeline (Figure 9.1).

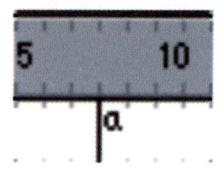

Figure 9.1 An 'a' is displayed in keyframes containing actions

Action types

There are two types of action in Flash:

1. Frame actions.
2. Button actions.

The first refers to actions that need no user input to generate the action. When the movie reaches a particular action frame in its playback it carries out the instruction. Individual frames can each contain many actions. A button action, on the other hand, requires input from the user before it carries out the instruction.

Frame actions

An action is assigned to a frame from the **Frame Actions** dialog box, accessed as usual by **right-clicking** on the frame and selecting **Actions** (Figure 9.2).

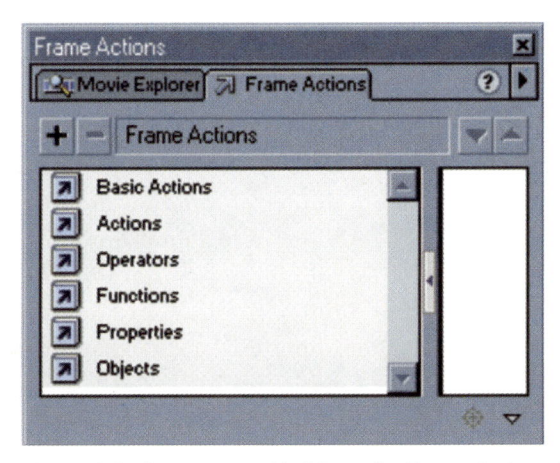

Figure 9.2 Actions are added from the Frame Actions dialog box

By clicking on one of the action classes, you can bring up a menu of available commands (Figure 9.3).

We'll look at these actions in more detail later on. But once you have selected a keyframe, double-clicking on any one of these actions will copy it to the right-hand panel and bring up a parameters box below (Figure 9.4).

Figure 9.3 Bringing up the Actions menu

You can keep adding actions to this one frame so that you could, for example, turn on anti-aliasing to improve the quality of the playback, stop all sounds which might still be playing from previous instructions and then jump to

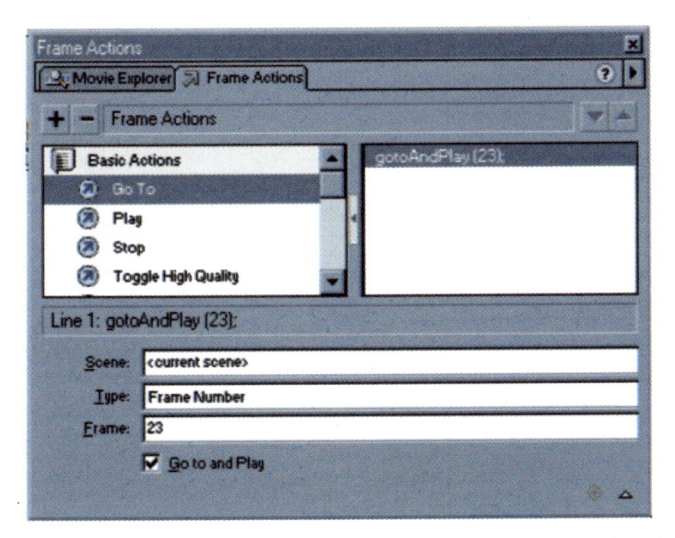

Figure 9.4 The parameters for the action appear below the listed action

If you can't see the associated parameters box, click on the little arrow in the bottom right-hand corner of the Frame Actions dialog box to expand the dialog view.

another frame. This sequence is shown in Figure 9.5. You can remove previously inserted actions by highlighting the particular action and then clicking on the '-' button.

Note on the right-hand side of the actions list there are up and down buttons. These let you alter the order in which the actions are carried out. Flash always starts from the top of the list and works its way downwards. So, for instance, if there were two instructions – one of which took you to another frame and the second of which took you to a new URL (uniform resource locator or, more

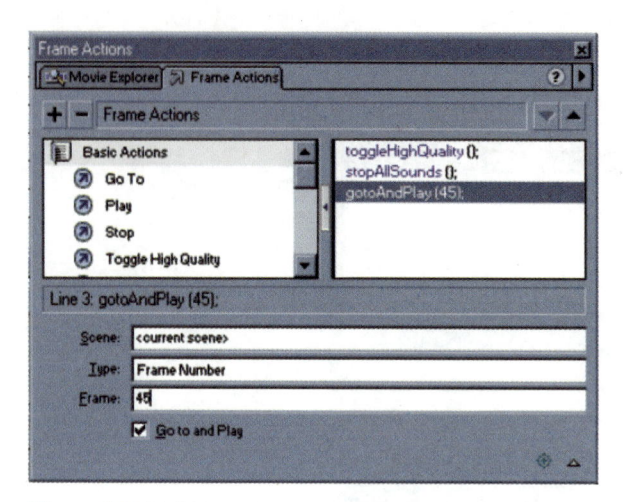

Figure 9.5 Multiple actions can be assigned to one frame

simply, web page address) – then if the former were at the top of the list you would always be taken to the new frame, while if the latter headed up the action list you would always be redirected to the new URL.

Frame labels and comments

Although you can easily tell Flash to jump to a particular frame from one of your action frames, it is often better (especially in longer movies) to give your target frame a label and to instruct Flash to jump to the label rather than the frame number. If you were to insert or delete frames after specifying a frame number you might have to redefine your jumps, so the use of labels obviates this.

Sometimes, too, for frames that are not the targets of action frames, it is useful to add comments about the frame that describe what is happening. This often makes it easier at a later date to pick up from where you left off programming the movie.

Flash allows you to place either labels or comments on any frame, but you cannot add both to one frame. You add them by going to the Frame Panel dialog box and inserting a label into the **Label** box (Figure 9.6).

Figure 9.6 Add labels via the Frame Panel

You add a comment in exactly the same way, but precede your text with two slashes ('//'), as shown in Figure 9.7.

When you add a label, the Timeline will add a little red flag to the frame and display as much of the label as it can. A comment will instead have the effect of adding two green slashes as well as the comment to the Timeline representa-

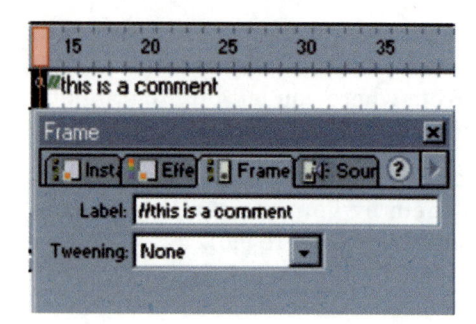

Figure 9.7 A comment begins with two slashes

tion. Sometimes there may not be room to see the entire comment or label because of a following keyframe, but you can always see a 'tool tip' associated with a label or comment when you hover over the Timeline frame (Figure 9.8).

Figure 9.8 Hover over a Timeline frame to see the contents of a comment or label

Some basic actions

We saw in Figure 9.3 that there are plenty of actions that you can associate with a particular frame. We'll consider just three of them for the moment.

9: Interactivity

The **Stop** and **Play** actions are two of the most fundamental. You add these to any frame to control the playback of the movie at particular points. You might want, for instance, a moving animation to begin and then pause until such time as another action is completed, and then resume. You can also override the playback defaults of the finished Shockwave format (.swf) file or projector file – both of which we'll be examining in Chapter 12 – to make them play or pause when they start up.

When you add either of these actions, there are no additional parameters to enter (Figure 9.9).

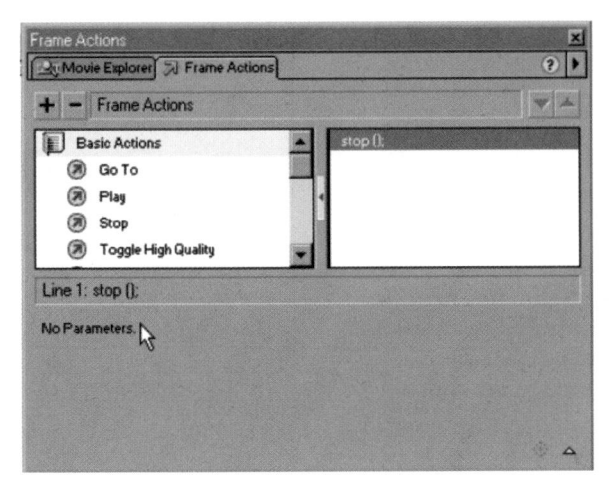

Figure 9.9 Neither Stop nor Play actions need additional parameters

Unlike the use of Stop and Play, the **Go To** action needs you to enter additional parameters for Flash to know what you want it to do. To make Flash resume playing once it has reached a new location, make sure the check box that reads **Go to and Play** is ticked (which you can see at the bottom of Figure 9.10). From the parameters area at the bottom, you can choose which scene to go to (assuming you have more than one, that is!) and which frame to go to (you can choose to go to a frame by its frame number or by a label).

Say, for instance, that we wish our action frame to whisk us away to a frame called *blodwyn* which is in scene 3. Figure 9.10 shows us what the action parameter box would look like.

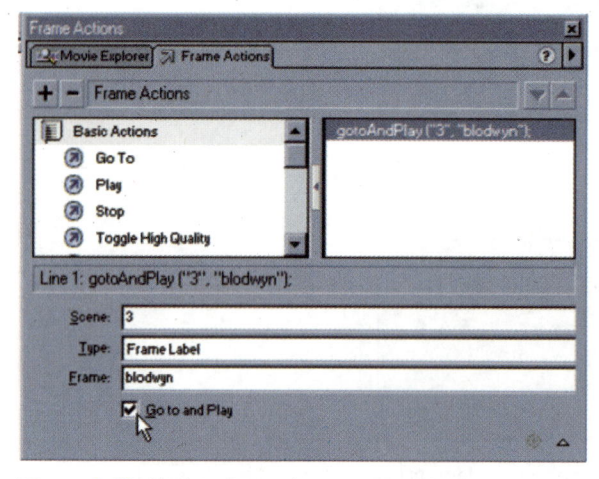

Figure 9.10 Flash is directed to jump to 'blodwyn' in scene 3 from this action frame, and then to start playing straight away

We'll look at some of the expression possibilities later on.

To try out your specified actions, you can use the **Test Movie** or **Test Scene** options in the **Control** menu. If you try simply using **Enter** in editing mode the actions will, by default, be disabled; this is to stop you being whisked off to destinations unknown when you are trying to work on a specific part of the timeline. You can, however, switch on the actions by going to your **Control** menu and clicking on **Enable Simple Frame Actions** (Figure 9.11).

There is no reason why you could not specify the name of a frame or scene, even if it has not yet been defined – as long as you are organised enough to know in advance what your naming conventions are going to be!

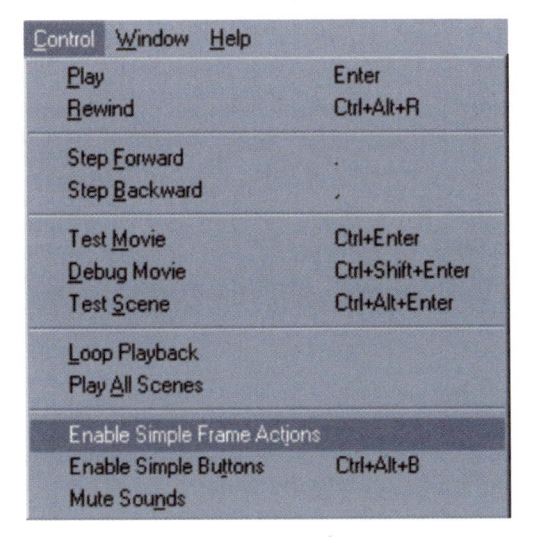

Figure 9.11 Enabling the editor to preview your actions

Buttons

One of the most basic ways in which you can get your audience to participate in the running of your movie is to allow them to interface with the movie by using buttons.

Buttons are basically symbols that can display a different image for each of the possible states. A button can only ever have four frames associated with it and these are:

1. The **Up** state – which represents the button when the mouse cursor is not over the button.
2. The **Over** state – which occurs when the mouse cursor is hovering over the button.
3. The **Down** state – which shows what the button looks like when it is clicked.
4. The **Hit** state – which you never see within the final movie, but which defines an area over which the button will respond.

It is perfectly acceptable to include movie clips within different button frames to display animated buttons.

Creating a button

Simple buttons are easily created using basic geometric shapes. If you change characteristics of the shapes within the different button states, it will be easy for your audience to know that your shapes are actually buttons.

Start by creating a symbol by going to your **Insert** menu and selecting **New Symbol** (Figure 9.12).

9: Interactivity 161

Figure 9.12 Insert a new symbol from the *Insert* menu

In the resulting properties dialog box you can specify a new name for your symbol if you like, but you must select **Button** behaviour (Figure 9.13).

A Timeline for your button is created, offering you the four standard states (Figure 9.14).

Initially the button has only one empty keyframe in its 'Up' state. Select this frame and then create some graphic on the stage to represent the up state of

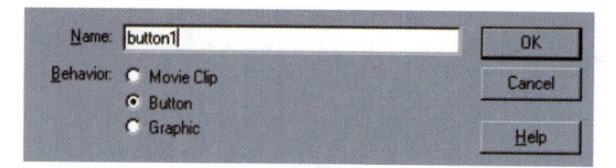

Figure 9.13 Set the symbol behaviour to *Button*

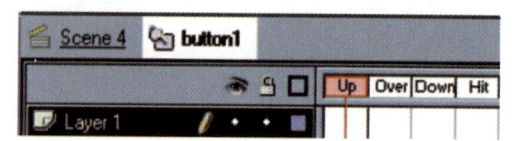

Figure 9.14 Flash creates four states for your new button

the button. It's useful to remember that the crosshair in the middle of the Stage gives you a fixed point of reference to work from.

For this example, we'll choose to place a filled circle as our basic button (Figure 9.15). Once that has been placed we click on frame 2 and make it a keyframe (using **right-click**). For our 'Over' state we can change its colour fill. (Duplicating the previous keyframe means we can get our alignments sorted out.)

For the 'Down' state we once again convert frame 3 into a keyframe and change the fill colour again, but this time we can simulate the button being 'pushed in' if, with the button state selected, we hit the down and right arrow keys once each.

The 'Hit' state doesn't worry about what colours are used. It is only to guide Flash as to which area of the Stage belongs to the button's area of influence. Some people feel comfortable having the entire 'hit' state depicted in some colour such as cyan so that they can immediately recognise it when they see it. For this example we'll once again fill the circle. The fact that the 'Hit' state is slightly bigger than the overall button helps the user to determine the button's area.

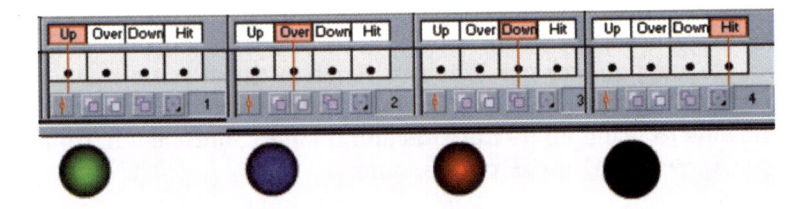

Figure 9.15 The four basic button shapes

Once the button has been completed you need to return to movie editing mode. A copy of your button will be placed in the library and it is from here that you can place an instance of it onto your Stage area.

There is absolutely no reason why you should stick to the same shaped graphic for each of your button states. You could have, for instance, a square, a circle and a star for the three 'Up', 'Down' and 'Over' states – just so long as your 'Hit' state is large enough to cover the entire area of the three other states.

An easy way to ensure your 'Hit' state is large enough is to **Edit:Copy** and **Edit:Paste in Place** each of the initial three states into the 'Hit' keyframe. That way you can be sure that each of the different shapes is effectively

*Just as when you set frame actions, Flash by default switches off the option of allowing you to view the button states in editing mode. If it didn't, you would find great difficulty in repositioning them or working with them. But to switch off this default you do virtually the same as for frame actions. Go to your **Control** menu, but this time select **Enable Simple Buttons**. However, it is usually best to test your buttons by going to **Control:Test Scene**.*

There is absolutely no reason why the 'Hit' state of a button needs to be in the vicinity of the rest of the button. Nor why there should be only one hot spot. You could have hot spots dotted around the Stage if you really wanted to!

recognised when you mouse-over the button. You could even use the **Modify:Shape:Expand Fill** by a pixel or two, making the 'Hit' area slightly bigger than necessary so that the button is activated when the mouse cursor is near the actual button.

Interactivity with buttons

Now that we have learned the basics about creating buttons, they can be used for helping the user to interact with your movie. Apart from the normal 'Up', 'Down' and 'Over' states, you can get Flash to react to these same mouse cursor events by completing certain actions. If you **right-click** on the button instance you will be able to bring up its **actions** and it's here, once again, that you can set what are known as **MouseEvent** actions.

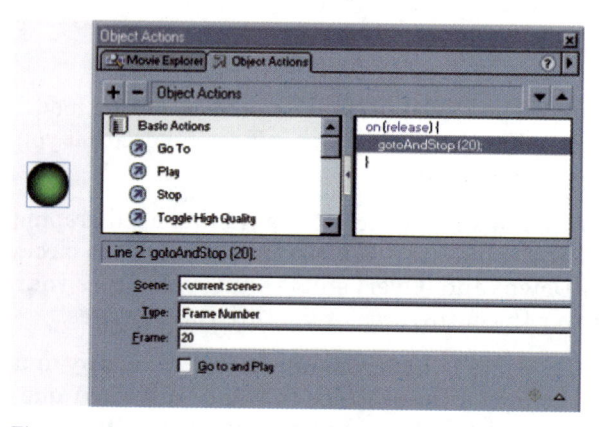

Figure 9.16 Assigning actions to buttons from the Instance Properties dialog box

9: Interactivity

As before, we click on the '+' button or double-click on the action to add actions (Figure 9.16) – let's choose 'Go To'. Here, we assign the button to jump the action to frame 20 of the current frame. This time Flash adds the lines:

```
On (Release)
Go to and Stop (20)
End On
```

On (MouseEvent)s

All button actions are structured in this way. The 'On (MouseEvent)' and '}' lines enclose what it is Flash must do when the button is activated.

Although Flash defaults to the 'On (Release)' command, you can just as easily set the action to occur on any of eight MouseEvent occurrences. As you can see in Figure 9.17, you are offered a number of options.

If you want to add events within the 'On (MouseEvent)' and '}' tags, highlight the line above where you want to add an event and then click on the '+' button. The new action will be added immediately below this highlighted line.

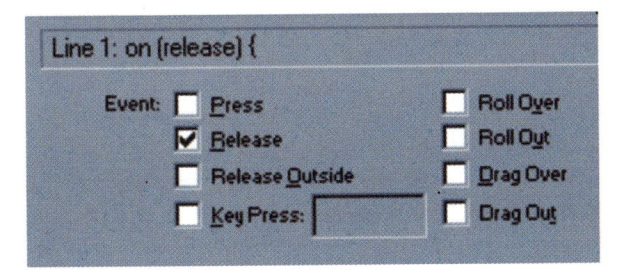

Figure 9.17 Change the value of 'MouseEvent' by clicking in one of the boxes

1. **Press:** occurs when the button is clicked downwards.
2. **Release:** occurs when the button is released after it has been clicked down, but only if the cursor is still in the button area. If the button is clicked and then the mouse dragged off the button before being let go, the action will not happen.
3. **Release Outside:** is the opposite of Release, in that the mouse must be outside the button's area before being released after clicking, otherwise the action will not happen.
4. **Key Press:** occurs whenever a specified key is pressed. The user does not have to use the mouse for this event to occur, however, and the mouse cursor does not have to be anywhere near the button in question. Simply, the button must be 'visible' somewhere on the Stage.
5. **Roll Over:** will occur any time that the mouse invades the button's 'Hit' area.
6. **Roll Out:** occurs whenever the mouse rolls out of the button's active area.
7. **Drag Over:** works when the user holds down the mouse within the button area, rolls the cursor outside of the active area and then returns within that area.
8. **Drag Out:** happens when the mouse button is pressed over the button, and the pointer is then moved out of the active area.

So, buttons can get your movie to react in different ways, depending on whether, for instance, you click the button or move the cursor over the button, or even press a key on the keyboard.

When you assign actions from the action list as shown in Figure 9.17, there is no reason why you cannot stack them so that, for instance, you can issue one

9: Interactivity

set of commands dependent on **on(rollOver)** and another one on **on(rollOut)** and a third on **on(release)** (Figure 9.18).

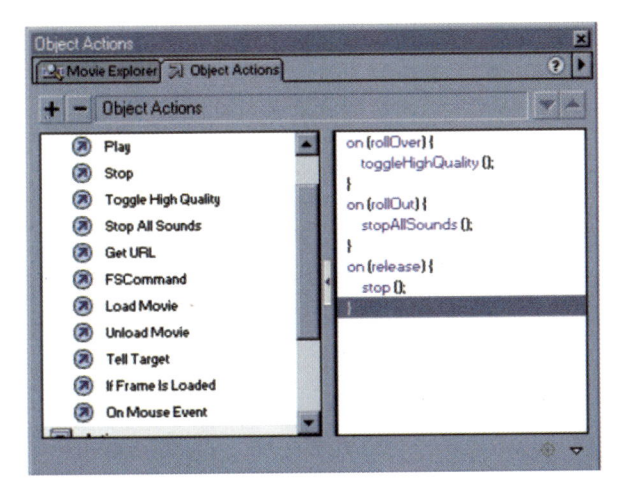

Figure 9.18 Multiple-choice actions

*Buttons don't actually have to have any graphics on them at all. Instead you could use what are referred to as **Invisible Buttons**. As long as the 'Hit' frame has content, you can ask your users to click anywhere within an area of the screen to launch the next action. This might be useful if, for instance, you wanted to pause an interactive presentation and let your users resume play simply by clicking anywhere.*

Sound 10

How Flash handles sounds

Importing sounds

Adding sounds to frames

Adding sounds to buttons

Sync settings

Streaming sounds

Making simple edits to your sound files

How Flash handles sounds

Just as the arrival of pictures on web sites revolutionised the entire way in which the world wide web was used, and was the main reason that its use grew in such a spectacular fashion, so too is the use of sound on web sites becoming all-pervasive across the Internet.

Flash can handle sounds that have been recorded in WAV and MP3 formats. MP3 files are, by definition, smaller than WAV files because of their in-built compression, and if you can you should import these in preference to WAV. Additionally, if you have QuickTime v4 on your computer, you can import Sun AU and QuickTime sound files.

Sounds can be used either as one-off events (such as a click sound when a button is pressed) or as a streaming sound that, for instance, delivers background music as your movie progresses. These two types of sound are handled differently by Flash and it is important to understand where the main differences lie:

- An **event** sound has to download completely before it can play. It will then keep on playing until instructed to stop.
- A **streaming** sound starts to play as soon as enough information has been downloaded for the first few frames. Thereafter the sound is synchronised to the Timeline as Flash forces the frames to keep in pace with the sound. If the frames take too long to draw, Flash drops some of the frames in order to keep up.

Importing sounds

You import sounds in exactly the same way you would import bitmaps and other artwork. From the **File** menu choose **Import** and select the file type to read **WAV**, **MP3** or **All Sound Formats** before selecting your particular sound (Figure 10.1).

*You can import as many sound files as you like in one go by holding down the **<Ctrl>** key as you select the different files.*

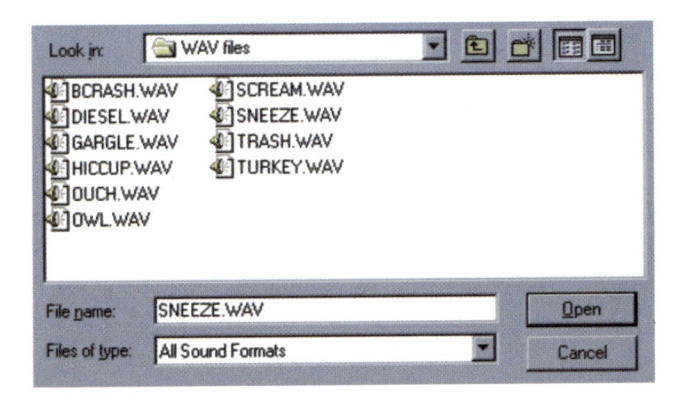

Figure 10.1 Importing WAV files

Flash imports the files directly into its library for you to use as required. Remember, you can inspect the contents of your library by selecting **Window:Library** (or **<Ctrl> L**) and in the preview window you will see the waveform for each selected sound file. Clicking on the play button allows you to hear what the file sounds like (Figure 10.2).

Although there is nothing to stop you adding sounds to graphics layers, you will find it easier to allocate separate layers to individual sounds and to keep these layers together so that you can easily find particular sounds when it's time to update or edit them.

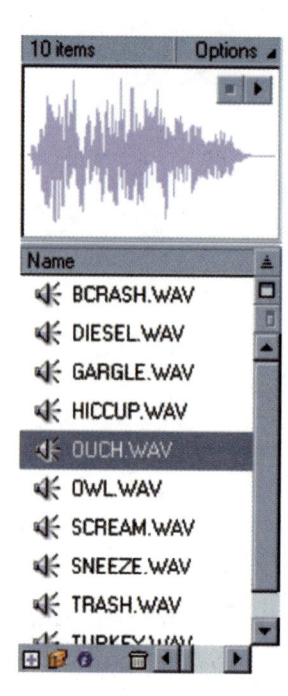

Figure 10.2 You can 'preview' your sound files directly in the library window

Flash does not, of itself, group all sound layers together, but you can cheat by creating a mask layer and adding the sound layers as 'masked layers', thereby creating a hierarchy (Figure 10.3). Because there are no graphics to worry about in these layers, the fact that they are masked makes no difference to the playback of your sound files.

10: Sound 173

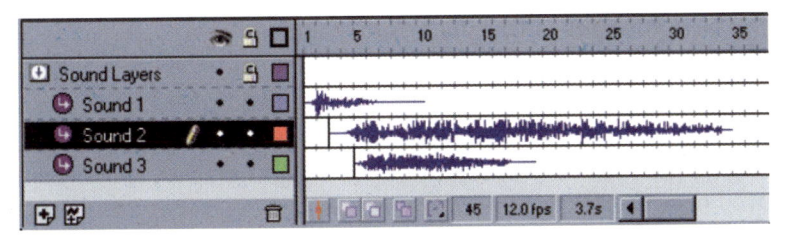

Figure 10.3 Add sound layers as marked layers for easy identification

Adding sounds to frames

You can assign any sound that is in your movie's library by dragging it to the Stage once you have selected, or created, a keyframe. It obviously doesn't matter where you drop the sound file on the Stage since the sound is 'invisible', but you will see a sound symbol outline as you drop the file onto the Stage and Flash will attach that sound file to the particular keyframe you have selected.

Apart from adding a sound instance by dragging it from the Movie's library (**Window:Library**), you can also add it by calling up the **Window:Panels: Sound** dialog box. You can then inspect the sound drop-down menu to select the sound from the movie's library (Figure 10.4).

*You can enlarge the height of individual layers and by doing so it is possible to see more of the waveform of the sounds for better placing your graphics and action files. To enlarge a layer within your Timeline, select **Modify:Layer** and set your layer height to **100%** (normal), **200%** or **300%**.*

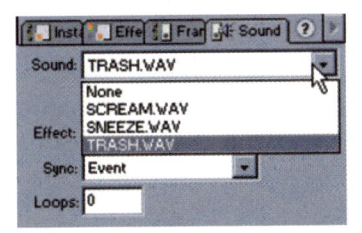

Figure 10.4 Selecting a sound from the Sound Panel dialog box

We'll return to the other options in this dialog box in a short while.

Adding sounds to buttons

It can be very useful for your viewers to have sounds allocated to your buttons. Apart from adding a touch of reality, they can help to highlight hot spots when the cursor is moved over them.

With your button visible on the Stage, **right-click** on it and choose **Edit** to open it up in symbol-editing mode. Add a new layer in the button's Timeline and label it **Sounds**. We now want to assign two sounds to the button – one when the user's cursor hovers over it and another when the button is actually clicked.

First, then, you need to **Insert:Blank Keyframes** into both the **Over** and **Down** states. Then you assign sounds to each of these two keyframes in the way we have just described. You should see a Timeline similar to that shown in Figure 10.5.

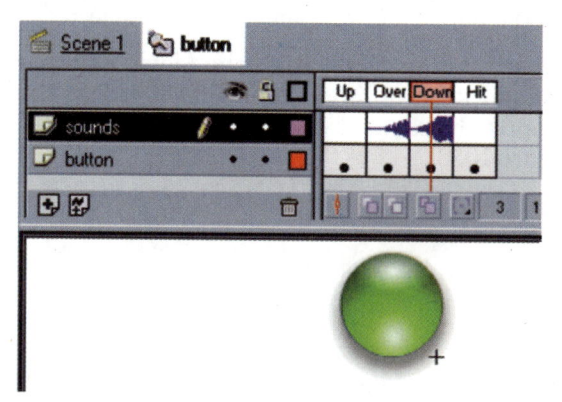

Figure 10.5 Adding sounds to a button

Once you are happy with the placing of the sounds, you can return to movie-editing mode by clicking on the **Scene** button shown at the top left of Figure 10.5. Remember that you can only 'preview' the sounds by first selecting **Control:Enable Buttons**.

Sync settings

We saw in Figure 10.4 that there were other drop-down menus which were pertinent to the way that sounds played along the Timeline. If we begin by looking at the Sync drop-down menu, we can see there are four options (Figure 10.6):

1. Event
2. Start
3. Stop
4. Stream.

There is no reason why you cannot allocate sounds to the 'Up' and 'Hit' states of the button. In these cases, you would hear the particular sounds when you either rolled the cursor out of the button's area, or when you released the button within the active 'hit' area.

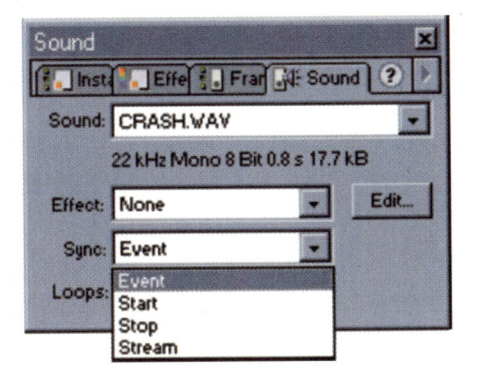

Figure 10.6 Choosing a Sync setting

By default, Flash sets a sound to play as an 'Event'. This means that the beginning of the sound is set to a particular keyframe, regardless of what is happening around it in the rest of the movie.

This can impact your movie in two dramatic ways. For instance, as all the information to play an *event* sound is contained within a specific keyframe, Flash will pause to download all the sound information from that particular frame and only then continue with the rest of the movie. This means that you should only use short sounds as event sounds, otherwise your movie could become jerky as it stops and starts waiting for long sounds to download.

Another aspect of the event choice is that if a sound is longer than the overall length of the section of your movie in which it is contained, it will keep on playing even after that section has come to an end. The way to stop this happening is to insert a **Stop** command.

Choose where you want your particular sound to stop and insert a blank keyframe. Although this has the effect of cutting off your view of the waveform in the Timeline, the sound will continue to play. However, if you now go to the sound panel dialog box for this blank keyframe, you can specify in the **Sync** menu to stop the sound and also specify the name of the particular sound you want stopped.

To let you know a Stop command has been issued, Flash places a small square in the Timeline where the sound ends (Figure 10.7).

Adding two sounds simultaneously

Flash can play as many sounds simultaneously as you like. However, only one sound can be assigned to each keyframe, so this means that if you want two sounds to start at the same frame, each must be assigned to a separate layer.

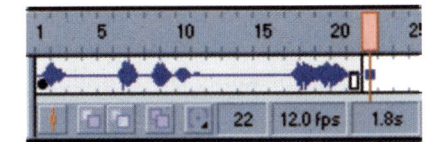

Figure 10.7 A Stop command is shown by the little black square

(Remember, though, that the more sounds Flash has to download, the longer will be the pause at this particular frame.)

Alternatively, if you want one sound to start after another but for both sounds to be playing simultaneously, it is quite in order for the two sounds to be placed on the same layer, as long as they are not instructed to start in the same frame.

Start sounds
At first encounter, it appears that *Start* sound has an almost identical behaviour pattern to *Event* sound. After all, the sound is set in train when a specific keyframe is encountered.

The important difference, however, is that with a *Start* sound instruction, only one instance of this sound can play at any one time, whereas with an *Event* sound, you can have multiple instances of the same sound playing simultaneously.

This means that if, for instance, a movie is set to loop and the sound that kicks off in the first loop playback is still playing when this frame repeats, then:

- if the sound is an *Event* sound you will hear two instances of the sound playing simultaneously (but not necessarily in sync);

We referred just now to the scene looping. And just as a scene or movie can loop (when frame actions are set this way), so too can a sound be made to loop a specific number of times. If you look at Figure 10.4 you will see there is a dialog box in which you can specify the number of times a sound should loop.

- if the sound is a *Start* sound, only the first instance will play, and there will be no repeat until such time as the first instance of the sound has stopped and the scene has looped again to hit the keyframe containing the sound.

Streaming sounds

Unlike *Event* sounds that must be completely downloaded before they can play, **Streaming Sounds** start playing once only a fraction of the information has downloaded. By setting the **Sync** to **Stream**, Flash synchronises it with specific frames of your movie and plays the sound until either a new keyframe is encountered or a Stop command is issued.

In Streaming Audio, Flash subdivides the sound into clips whose length is proportional to the overall frame rate. So, if the frame rate is set to the default of 12 frames per second, each clip of sound is created to last $\frac{1}{12}$th of a second. Each of these subclips is timed to start with each new frame encountered, but if the sound is too fast for the images, Flash sacrifices some of the frames to keep up with the sounds. This could have the effect of making the movie look jerky, but that is simply one of the downsides to streaming audio against a fixed frame rate.

With streaming sounds, you can hear how the sound interacts with the different frames by 'scrubbing' along the Timeline. Drag the playhead across the Timeline and see how the sound peaks coincide with different aspects of the frame contents (Figure 10.8).

If the synchronisation is not to your liking, you can add or delete frames to get the timing better. This can be made simpler if you switch between different views in your **Edit Envelope** dialog box, which can be accessed by clicking on

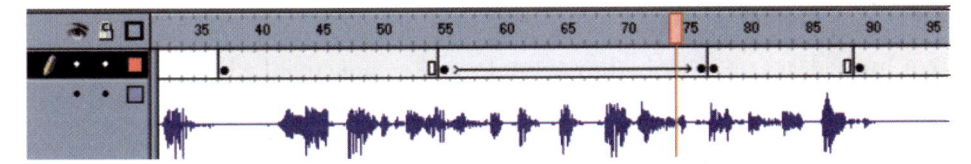

Figure 10.8 'Scrubbing' along the Timeline

the **Edit** button in the sound panel. You can view the sound sequence in either frame view or time view by clicking on one of the right-hand icons at the bottom of the edit envelope (Figure 10.9) and thereby deduce exactly how many frames you need to add or delete to make your sound file fit your frames sequence.

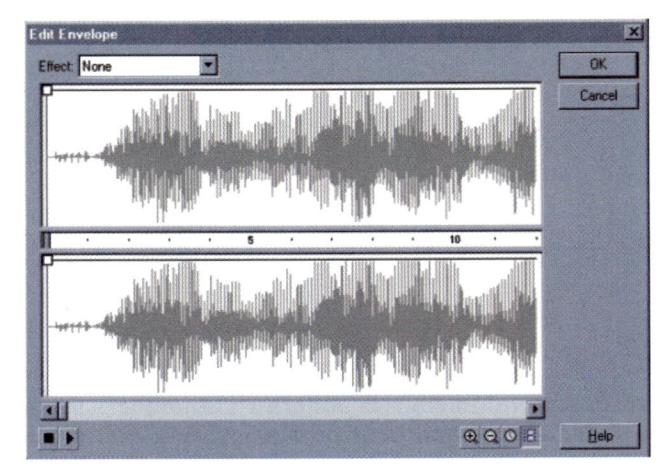

Figure 10.9 Frame view of the sound sequence in the Edit Envelope

Making simple edits to your sound files

To a limited degree, Flash allows you to make superficial edits to your sound files. You can alter:

- the start and end points of the sound;
- its volume;
- the relationship between the left and right stereo channels.

(However, for any serious editing it is probably better to edit the sound files in programs specific to the task.)

To change the volume of sound files with Flash, you begin by opening up the **Edit Envelope** as we did just a moment ago.

The **Effect** tab is where you can choose one of the following:

- None
- Left Channel
- Right Channel
- Fade Left to Right
- Fade Right to Left
- Fade In
- Fade Out
- Custom.

As you can see in Figure 10.10, the volume levels of both right and left channels can be set by dragging the envelope handles up or down. Choose one of the cross fade or fade in/out options, and the volume levels are set automatically.

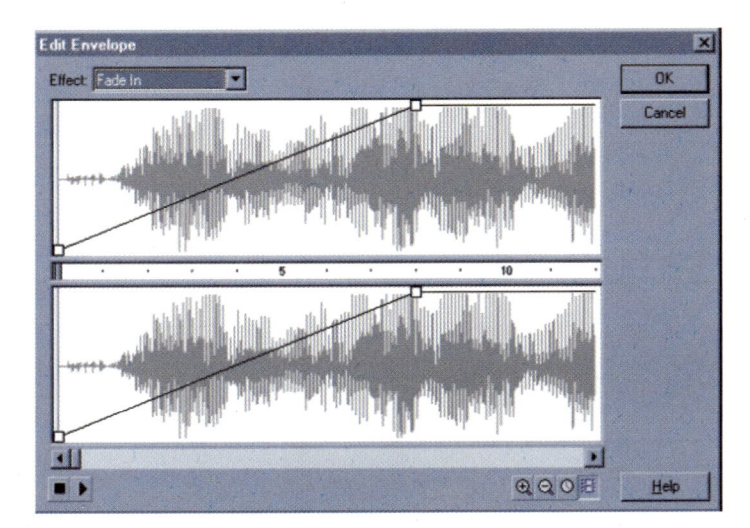

Figure 10.10 Setting a fade-in from the Edit Envelope dialog box

You can add more handles by clicking on the waveform – to a maximum of eight per channel – and each can then be dragged up or down, left or right, to change the volume levels along the playback line of the sound file (Figure 10.11).

To remove unwanted envelope handles you simply drag them from the window. To hear the resulting sound, click on the play icon shown in the bottom left-hand corner of Figure 10.11.

As we have already mentioned, Flash's sound editing is pretty basic, but it does allow for some simple effects. If you are likely to cut back the overall length of many of your sound files, it may still be worth doing so in an external sound-editing program since, although Flash can be set to ignore the start and end points of the sound, the overall file is still contained in the final Flash movie. This just takes up unnecessary space, making your final movie bigger than it needs to be.

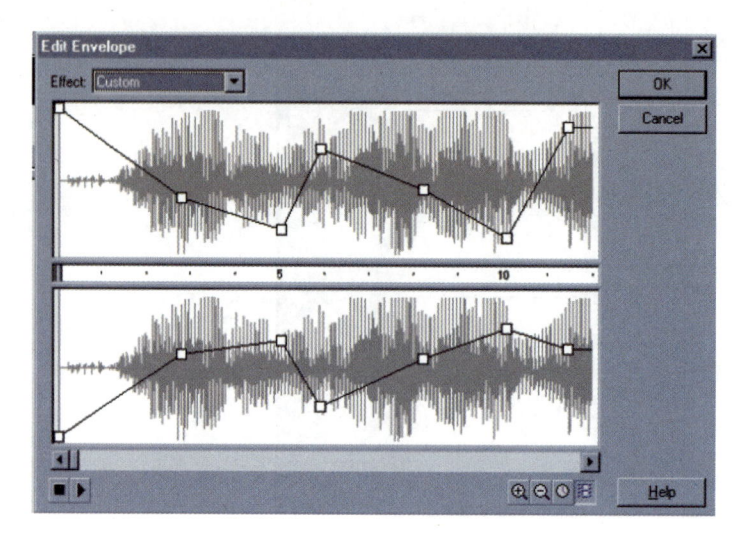

Figure 10.11 A sound file can contain up to eight handles – for each channel

Complex interactivity

11

ActionScript

Expressions and variables

Other actions

Conditions

Incorporating JavaScript

Debugging and commenting out your movie

Normal and Expert modes

Movie Explorer

Coloured prompts

We've seen how Flash allows you to interact with your movies in a number of ways – not least through the use of actions sparked off by clicking buttons or the choice of specific items on menus. With the arrival of version 4, Macromedia introduced complex interactivity into Flash for the first time; it introduced variables and expressions allowing the site designer to use formulaic interactivity that would test for certain conditions and carry out an action specific to the outcome of a particular test.

ActionScript

With Flash 5 Macromedia has made another major leap forward in introducing a scripting language based on JavaScript, which it calls *ActionScript*. If you are already familiar with JavaScript, ActionScript should not present you with too many problems. If you have not yet taken the plunge into this kind of programming, then ActionScript does its best to hold your hand along the way.

Using expressions and variables in Flash takes a little while to grasp, and many people find it much more difficult to come to grips with these than with other aspects of the design of a Flash production. However, we would strongly recommend working through the following pages, trying out the expressions for yourself and learning by experimentation. That way you should find that what appears daunting at first opens out a whole new vista for your site development and brings Flash into a realm of its own.

You will have seen from the relative sizes of the instruction manuals that ActionScript deserves a manual all to itself (weighing in with a 20% bigger volume than the rest of Flash put together!). So it would not be possible in a book this size to go into too much detail about everything on offer. However, by working through this chapter you will get a good idea of the kind of things that ActionScript can offer you and it should make experimentation with the remaining features that much simpler to grasp.

Expressions and variables

Let's start by defining exactly what we mean by these two basic building blocks.

An **Expression** is a type of formula made up of a mathematical combination of **variables**. Say you wanted to set a codeword made up from your birth date and another number set by the programmer. We could make it equivalent to the sum of the day of the month, the number of the month and the year in which you were born, plus the final number – 'X'.

So, if that birthday were the 13th February 1981 and the extra number was 4, the password would be 13+2+1981+4 = 2000.

Put as a mathematical expression we could say *Codeword = day + month + year + 'X'*. Here, *day, month, year* and *'X'* are all numerical variables.

Variables, which can be added or amended by the viewer of the movie, are called **concrete variables**. Variables that exist only in the inner workings of Flash, but over which the viewer has no control, are called **abstract variables**. So in the above example, *day, month* and *year* are concrete variables, while the *'X'* number is an abstract variable.

Concrete variable fields are added to a movie by selecting the **text options panel** and selecting **Input Text** from the drop-down menu (Figure 11.1).

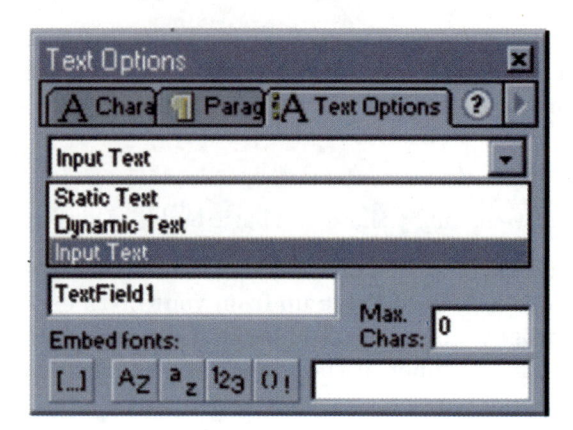

Figure 11.1 Selecting Input Text from the Text Options panel

Let's set up a very simple Flash scene that works out this codeword for us. Open up a new Flash document and select the text tool, making sure **Input Text** is selected (Figure 11.1). **Create** a text box and then **right-click** on it; select **Panels:Text Options**.

A dialog box similar to that shown in Figure 11.2 opens up. You will see a variable box, which is given the default name of **TextField1**, and this is where you give the text variable a name – so in this case overtype it with *'Day'*.

- The first of the check box options listed is labelled *HTML*. By ticking this, you are allowed to enter HTML tags into whatever text ends up in this variable, such as <B>, <I> or <FONT FACE> and so on.
- The next tick box forces a border round your text field. As you want the viewer to be able to see this box before they start typing in their details, we tick the box to make it show up.

11: Complex interactivity

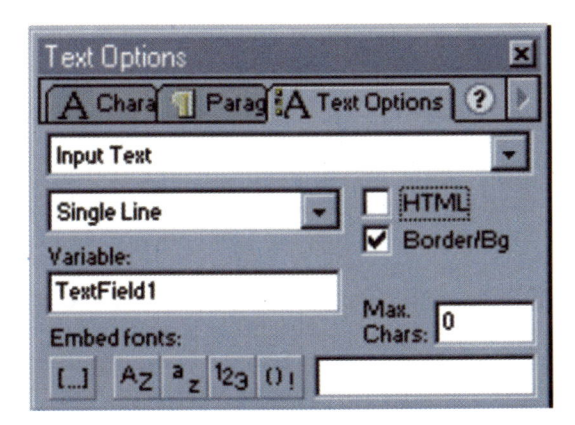

Figure 11.2 The text field properties dialog box is where you specify your variable properties

- The **single/multiline** entry allows the user to add as many lines of text as he likes, and to wrap that text to the width of the window. As we want the user to enter only a simple number this time we will leave this as *Single Line*. There is also a **Password** option in this menu, which allows you to force the user to enter a password (shown only as a series of asterisks) in order to be able to access another part of the movie.
- We can restrict the user to enter a **maximum number of characters** in the next field.
- The **Embed Font** options allow you to choose whether you want to save the font outlines with the published movie, and if so you can choose to select only uppercase, lowercase, numbers and so on. Selecting your outline options carefully can reduce the overall file size of your published movie.

Having set the options for the first of our text fields, we can add similar fields for the *month* and *year*.

In the first drop-down menu, there is another option from *Input* or *Static* text and that is **Dynamic Text** (Figure 11.3). Dynamic Text could be useful for inputting updateable text – for instance, using server-generated input from a program such as 'Generator', or text that changes dynamically with changing variables. But it is also useful if you want to stop people from editing something you have entered into a static text box but you also want a border round it so that it looks like all the other inputs. (All right! That's a very convoluted way round setting up your text field as a variable, which we'll come to in a moment, but please bear with us.) You can see that by using a Dynamic Text box we have been able to force a border, and we can choose whether to check **Selectable** depending on whether we want this field to be edited by the end users or not. We can do the same with our Codeword text box.

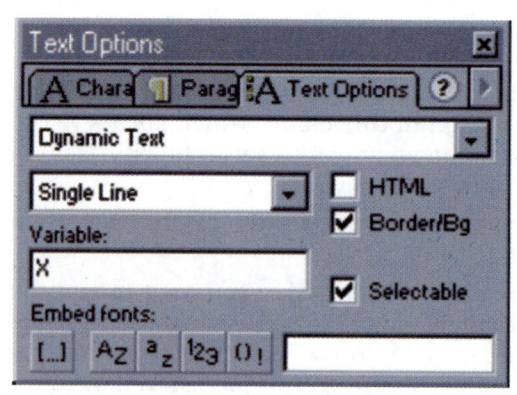

Figure 11.3 Dynamic Text is used where text will change according to variables and other input data

11: Complex interactivity

It will be helpful also if we were to put a text label beside each box so that when the user views the movie he knows which field is which (Figure 11.4)! Remember to set the text field modifiers as **Static text** when adding your labels.

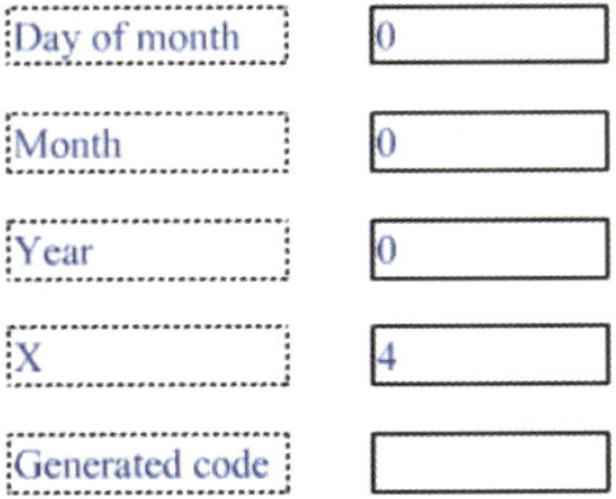

Day of month	0
Month	0
Year	0
X	4
Generated code	

Figure 11.4 Adding the text fields with their labels to the Stage

Having placed labels and text fields on the Stage, the next job is to specify the relationships between the different variable fields. Let's get Flash to generate our new codeword when we click on a button.

Place an instance of a button on the stage and right-click it to access its **Actions** dialog box. In the left-hand panel, click on **Basic Actions** to open up a list of ready-made actions for you to use. Find **Set Variable** and either drag it to the right-hand pane or double-click on it.

Straight away, a line of code appears which reads:

```
on{release}{
```

Flash is intuitive enough to know that you have assigned an action to a button, which means that it enters code based on the effect of doing something with a button. It opts for {release}, but you could force it to use another button state, as we saw in Chapter 9.

You are then presented with a couple of boxes to fill in:

1. You enter the name of the variable in the first box (in this case we have used **Code** as the variable for our codeword text box).
2. The value in this case is the sum of *day+month+year+x*. Note that we are expecting a numerical value, so the **Expression** checkbox is left unticked (Figure 11.5).

So we end up with the following lines of code:

```
on{release}{

code="day+month+year+x";

}
```

The final '}' denotes the end of the instruction beginning on{release}.

Now when we click the button, Flash should make the codeword equal to this sum of the variables. Try it out. But first ensure that in the **Control** menu, **Enable Simple Buttons** is ticked. Then click on **Control:Test Scene** (or **<CTRL> <Alt> Enter**) (Figure 11.6).

11: Complex interactivity   191

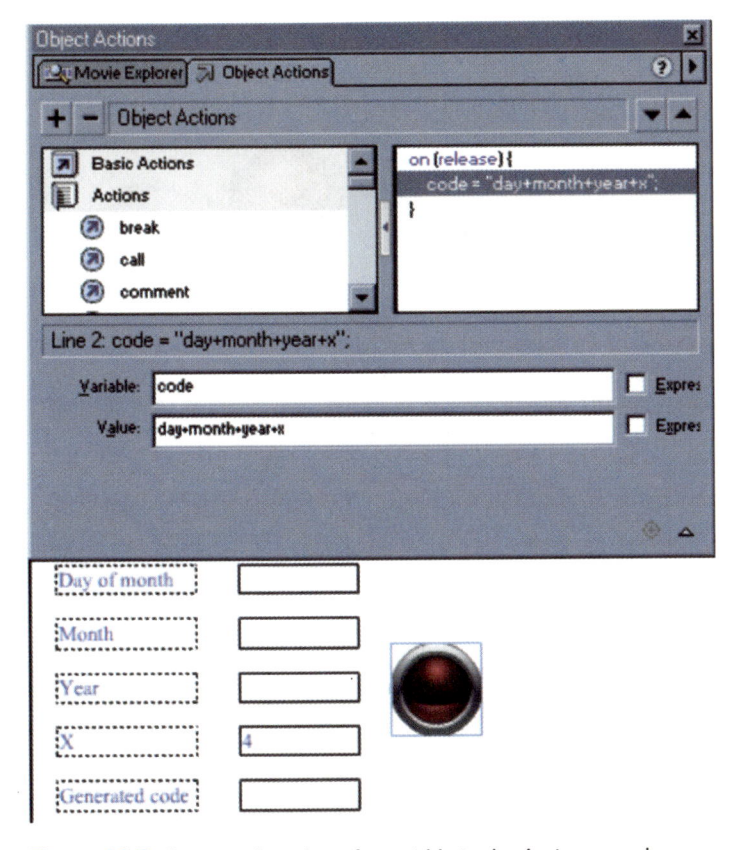

Figure 11.5 Entering the value of a variable in the Actions panel

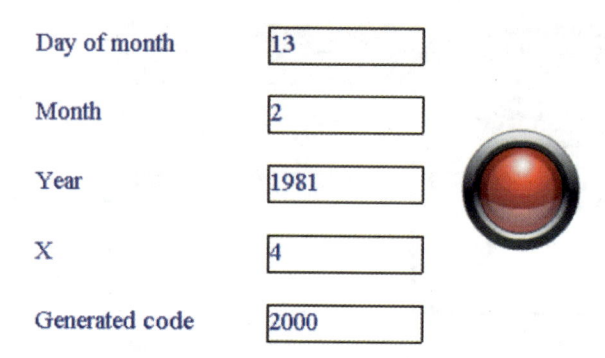

Day of month	13
Month	2
Year	1981
X	4
Generated code	2000

Figure 11.6 Testing the scene from the control menu ensures the expression has been entered correctly

Other actions

Apart from using simple expressions, we saw in Figure 11.5 that there are plenty of other options that we can choose from our Actions list.

Loading new files into your movie
The Actions menu has a couple of entries that allow you to load new files in to your movie or web site:

- **Get URL** is used to load a file into your browser window when the Flash file is played using a browser.
- **Load Movie** loads new movie files on top of your current movie so that the latter is either replaced by the former or complemented by another animation layer.

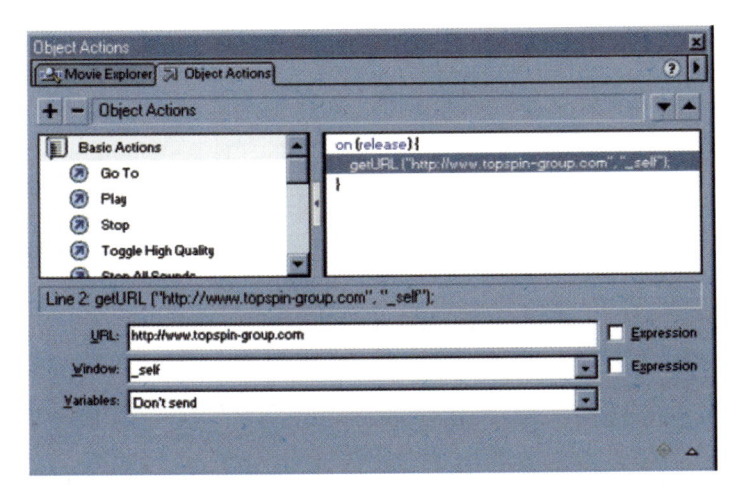

Figure 11.7 Entering a Get URL action

Get URL
In Figure 11.7, we have entered an absolute URL – *http://www.topspin-group.com*. Obviously, this is a text string, so we don't click on the **Expression** box. If we had, Flash would have come up with a warning (Figure 11.8) in glorious Technicolor that is impossible to miss!
The Window drop down-menu gives four choices:

1. **_blank** forces the new URL to be loaded into a new window.
2. **_self** specifies the current frame in the current window.
3. **_parent** loads the URL into the current frame's parent.
4. **_top** ensures the URL is loaded into the top-level frame within the current window.

URL is short for uniform resource locator, which in Internet terms is a way of specifying a web site address. An absolute URL gives information about the server on which the web site is located, the path to the web site itself and the name of the file being called. A relative URL, on the other hand, describes the address of the file relative to the page being displayed. When testing your movies on your computer, relative URLs allow you to specify files on your computer in relation to others rather than making you get onto the Internet to find an absolute address.

Flash 5 for Windows

The Get URL action command can also be used to send off information in an e-mail. In the URL box, enter **mailto:address** where 'address' is the e-mail address of the person you wish to e-mail. (So, to e-mail us you could insert mailto:info@topspin-group.com.) If you have two fields, one whose variable value is 'body' and the other 'subject', then the contents of the latter will be inserted into your e-mail message subject line, and the contents of body will be inserted into the e-mail body text.

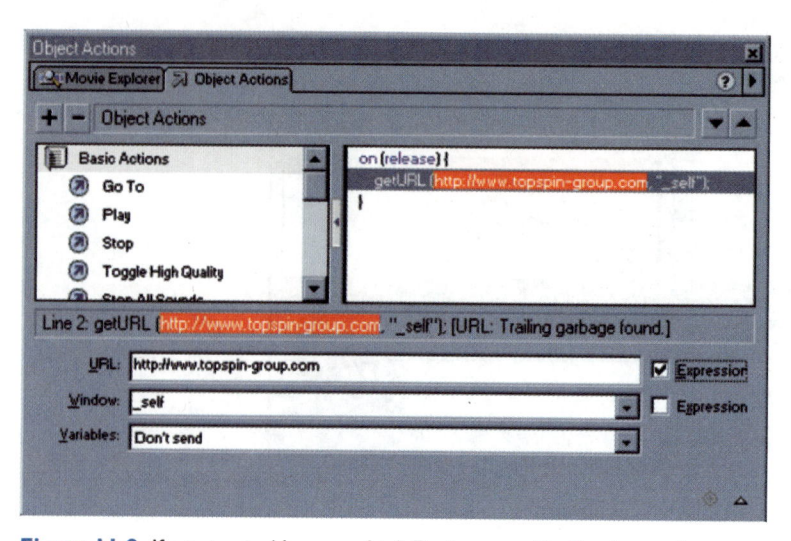

Figure 11.8 If you try to 'do a naughty', Flash acts as Big Brother and stops you doing so!

Finally, you can determine whether you want Flash to **GET** or **POST** variables (or not to pass any at all) to your URL address. This is useful if you need to send variables to a CGI script, which generates a .swf file as its CGI output. (We'll get more familiar with Shockwave – .swf – file formats in the next chapter.) If you aren't familiar with CGI commands you are probably best leaving this option set to *Don't Send*.

To test your Get URL action, go to the **File** menu and select **Publish Preview:HTML**. Your movie is exported as a .swf file, and an HTML file is created which embeds that .swf file. This HTML file is then opened up in the browser of your choice. Now when you click your button you should see the new URL page loaded into the frame specified in your Window drop-down menu (assuming you're connected to the Internet, of course).

Load movie

To load a new movie we choose the option **Load Movie** from the Object Actions menu (Figure 11.9). This action is used to play new movies without closing down the Flash player. For instance, if you wanted to play a series of banner adverts you could use a *Load Movie* action at the end of one .swf file to load the next movie sequentially. Alternatively, if you wanted to allow the user to choose from several .swf files, you could build an interactive branch to take the user to one .swf file or another depending on which button the user clicked.

Unlike the Get URL action above, we are offered the choice of setting the Level or Target for this action. Let's consider the Level setting first of all. By default, the movie that you are currently in is always in Level 0. Movies in levels higher than the present one are always loaded on top; so if, as in Figure 11.9, we specify Level 1 in this instance, we are instructing Flash to play the new movie on top of the present one. That means that if the new movie is located above the present one, it will obscure whatever is beneath it.

You can test the *Load Movie* action by choosing **Test Movie** from your **Control** menu.

Tell Target

Flash allows you to control a different movie clip from the one that is playing by using the action *Tell Target*. Its main use is in navigation where, by clicking

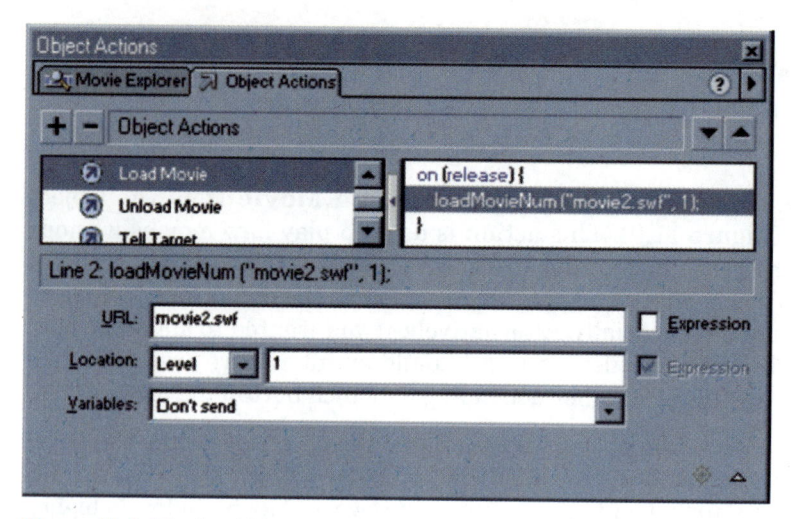

Figure 11.9 The Load Movie parameters box

on a button, you can instruct Flash to jump to a particular frame within a movie clip or to start a movie clip somewhere else on the stage.

For this example we will use one of the movie clips provided in Flash's common library – the biplane – and two buttons. We will get one of the buttons to stop the action of the plane's propeller, and the other button to start it again.

In order to be able to tell the buttons to carry out instructions on a particular movie clip, we have to give that clip a name. It is no good assuming that Flash can find the particular instance of the biplane because there may well be more than one instance of each clip.

So, on the Stage, select the instance of the biplane by right-clicking on it and then select **Panels:Instance**. A dialog box will appear as in Figure 11.10.

Figure 11.10 The Instance Panel dialog box

The lower box is an empty text field where we give this movie instance a unique name. We'll call it *plane*. By so doing, we can direct any button to target this particular instance of the movie clip, irrespective of how often the clip appears in our final movie.

Having given a unique identifier to the movie clip, we are able to start giving instructions to the buttons to perform specific actions. On the stage we place two button instances – *Stop* and *Play* (Figure 11.11).

Right-click on the Stop button to bring up its **Actions** panel. By double-clicking **Tell Target** (or dragging it to the right) Flash adds the following text to the actions list:

Figure 11.11 On the Stage we have our biplane with two buttons

```
on{release}{
tellTarget {""}
}
}
```

We now have to point the action to the correct movie clip. (As we only have one clip, this is easy!) As you can see in Figure 11.12, one can click on the penultimate button at the bottom right of the window for Flash to bring up a list of possible movie instances (Figure 11.13).

With the plane instance now selected, we call up the actions menu again and select **Stop**. Again, Flash updates the actions list (Figure 11.14).

We now do exactly the same for the second (play) button, but instead of adding *Stop* as our last action, we add **Play** (Figure 11.15).

11: Complex interactivity 199

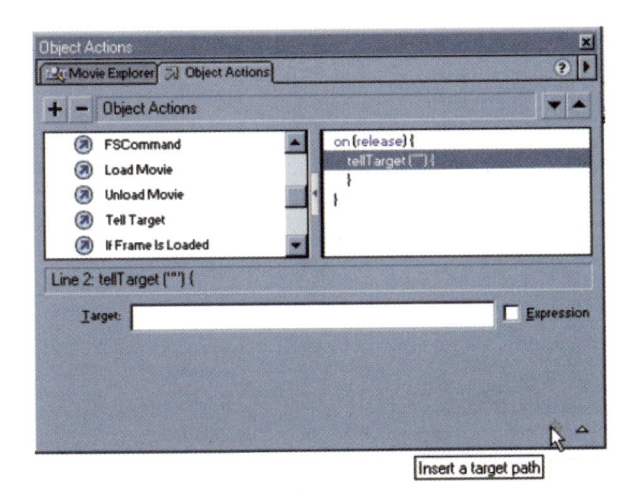

Figure 11.12 Here we instruct Flash to look for possible target instances

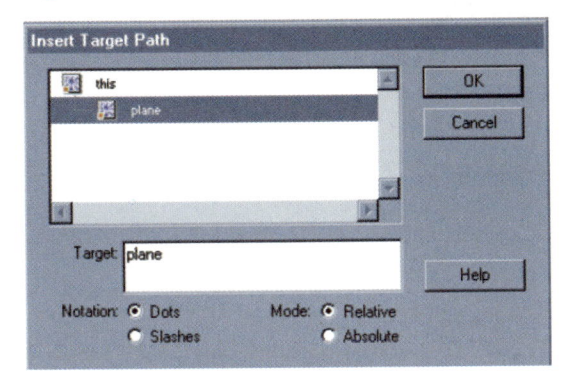

Figure 11.13 Flash lists 'all' the possible instances

Flash 5 for Windows

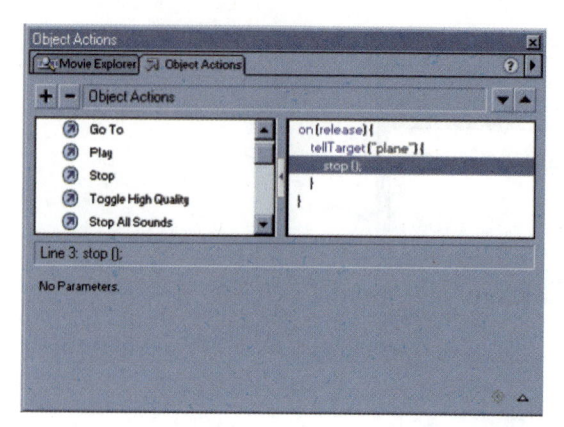

Figure 11.14 The complete actions list for the Stop button

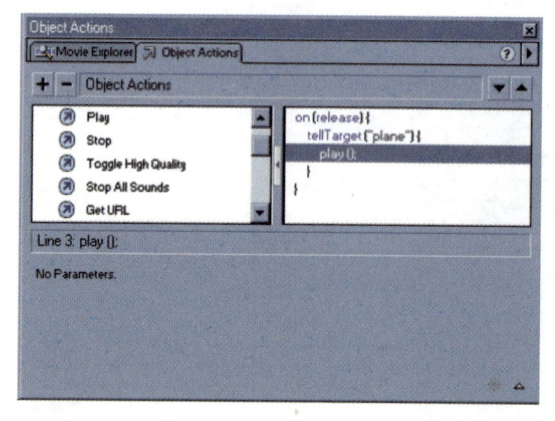

Figure 11.15 The dialog for the Play button

11: Complex interactivity

Now to see the Tell Target commands in action, we have to go to the **Control** menu and select **Test Movie**. Clicking on the **Stop** button stops the plane's propeller from rotating (Figure 11.16). The **Play** button starts it again.

Figure 11.16 Clicking on the Stop button halts the propeller of the plane

Conditions

There are two important conditional actions that you can use to test for the verity of statements or whether a certain condition has been met, and to act according to the result.

1. If frame is loaded.
2. If.

If frame is loaded
The first condition – *If frame is loaded* – speaks for itself. This is useful, for example, if you want to test whether data has been downloaded to the user's

computer before starting playback of a particular scene. If there is a great deal of animation you will get much smoother playback if the sequence has entirely downloaded first, rather than relying on the download to finish when the beginning is already playing. So, to keep your user amused while the rest of the movie clip is downloading you could have a teaser movie that repeats over and over until the signal is given that the rest of the movie has downloaded.

It is difficult to try out an example of this action on your computer, since the download time is likely to be far too fast for you to see the delay in action. Flash does try to simulate the streaming of movies (in your Flash Player go to **View:Show Streaming**) but it is still difficult to see the full effect. Suffice it to say that there are thousands of examples of such an action out on the world wide web where a splash screen appears which, at first glance, might appear to serve little useful purpose except to deny access to the main body of the site. In reality it's all rather like the proverbial swan on water: serene on top, but feverish activity underneath. While the splash screen diverts your attention, the movie is loading onto your computer out of sight until the condition is met to allow you access to it.

Testing for a downloaded movie clip is easy enough. In your Frame Actions dialog box, select **If Frame Loaded** and in the parameters section underneath enter the scene (if different from the current one) and the frame number (or frame label, preferably, if you have given labels to the different parts of your movie) (Figure 11.17).

Now you need to tell Flash what to do once the frame has loaded. We might, for instance, suggest that if frame 100 has been loaded the movie can start playing from frame 15. So, with the *If Frame Is Loaded* statement selected, we now add another action – in this case **Go To and play** – and in the parameters box give the frame number – 15 (Figure 11.17).

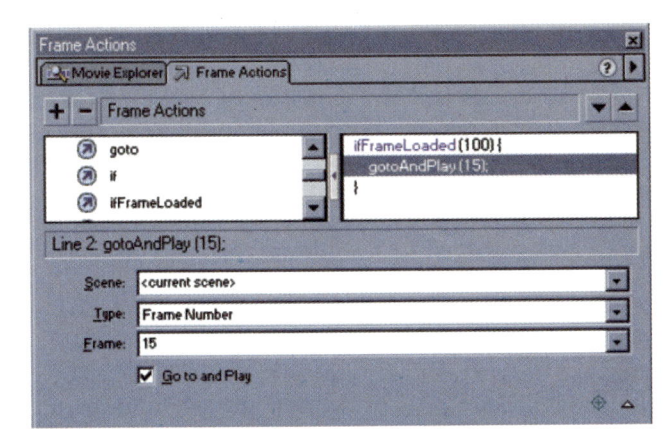

Figure 11.17 Defining *If Frame Is Loaded* actions

Looping an animation
Having created the conditional action to test if a frame has downloaded, it is likely you will want to loop your teaser animation until such time as the download is complete. The most straightforward way of doing this is to insert a **Go To** command at the end of your animation to instruct the clip to return to the first frame again. That way the clip repeats over and over again. If you then insert your *If Frame Is Loaded* condition you can instruct Flash to start the next movie clip once the condition has been met.

Looping has other uses, too. Using a conditional loop, you can test whether certain conditions are met and only when they are should Flash perform the next action.

For instance, you could set a variable – index – to equal 1. Every time the loop instructions are carried out, the index variable increases by 1. Only when index has a value equal to, or greater than, 10 will the loop condition be met and Flash can then move on to the next instruction. The simplest way to do this is to use the **While** command as shown in Figure 11.18. Here we have instructed Flash to keep the visibility of the biplane turned on until the index reaches 10. In practice this set of instructions will last hardly longer than the blink of an eye, since there are no other actions involved to slow down the loop. However, we have shown this purely as an illustration of the *While* loop.

If ... Else

Just as Loop statements can test for certain actions, so too can **If** and **If ... Else** statements. Using *If* you can choose to run an action only when a certain condition exists. You can use the logical operators offered by the Frame Actions box, if you wish, to help you construct your *If* statements. You can also nest a number of *If ... Else* statements to give alternative instructions if one condition is not met but another is.

For example, we could nest such statements so that a scene is played depending on which season of the year it is:

```
if (month="March" or "April" or "May") {
    gotoAndPlay ("spring", 1);
} else if (month="June" or "July" or "August") {
    gotoAndPlay ("summer", 1);
} else if (month="September" or "October" or "November") {
    gotoAndPlay ("autumn", 1);
```

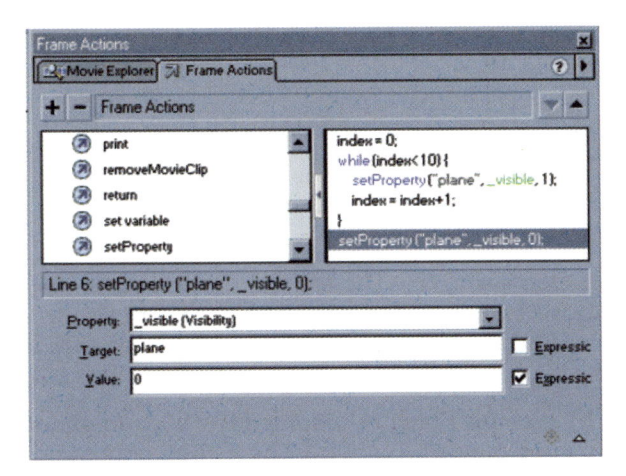

Figure 11.18 Using a While action to test for a condition

```
} else if (month="December" or "January" or "February") {
    gotoAndPlay ("winter", 1);
}
```

Incorporating JavaScript

Flash allows you to communicate with the browser hosting the Flash player, or the standalone projector. Using the **FS Command** statement, a message can be sent from Flash to the browser or projector, for instance, to cause the movie to fill the screen, to hide the menu bar or for opening message dialog boxes in a browser. Unfortunately, writing JavaScript routines is beyond the scope of this book, but the FS Command statement is given help from Flash for some of the basic commands such as in Figure 11.19.

Debugging and commenting out your movie

The problem with creating highly interactive movies is that the more complicated they get, the more likely it is that you will 'lose the plot' when it comes to making changes or corrections.

It is best when creating complex movies to test the actions continually as you go along. You can add comments, or explanatory notes, at any stage in the proceedings so that when you come to revisit a particular section at a later date it is immediately clear what each action is meant to do (Figure 11.20).

You can go further, however, by getting Flash to display information about what is going on when testing your movies. By using the **Trace** command, comments that you type into the Trace action's message parameter will appear in a new window as the action is carried out (Figure 11.21).

These comments will appear only when playing your movies in **Control:Test Movie** or **Control:Test Scene** modes; they will not appear, naturally, in your final published movie.

Normal and Expert modes

We've only been able to scratch the surface of ActionScript within Flash, but once you have started playing with some of the simpler commands it isn't nearly as daunting as when you are first presented with it. Or is it?

11: Complex interactivity   207

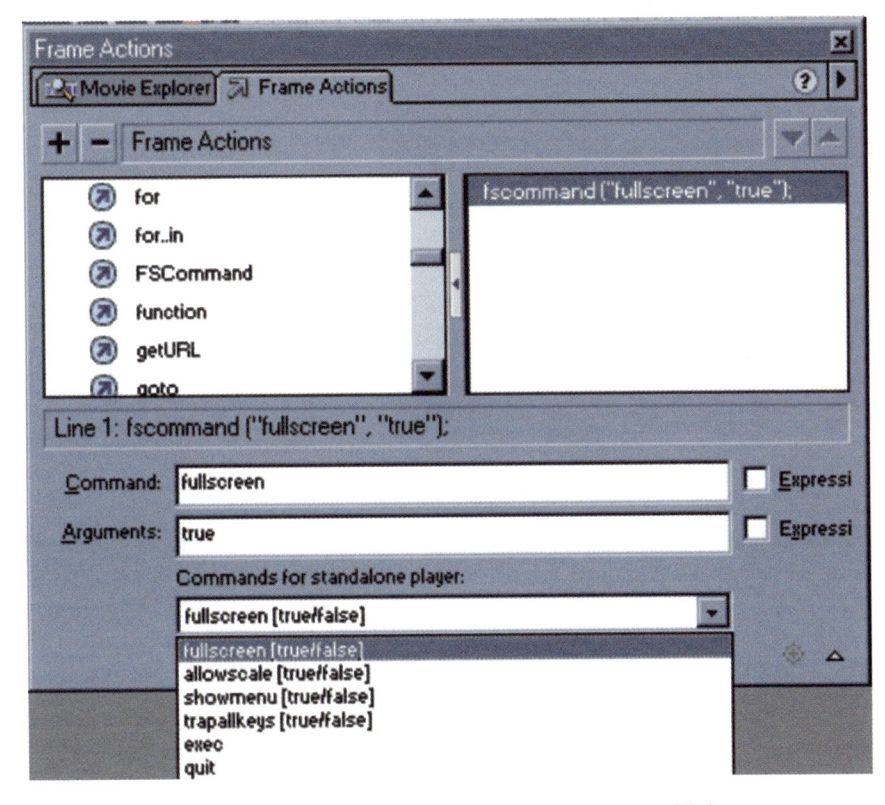

Figure 11.19 FS Command can be used to cause the projector to fill the screen

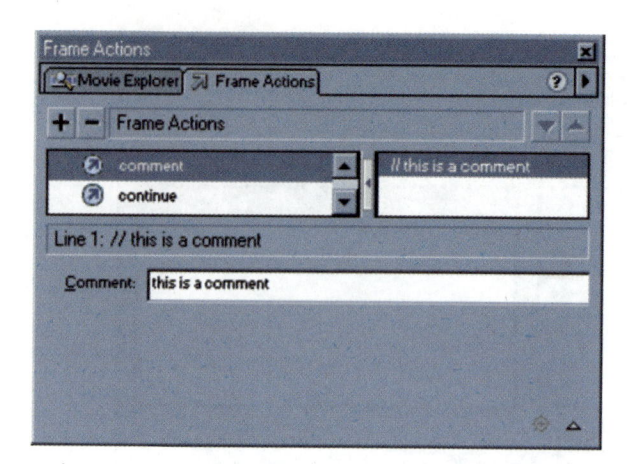

Figure 11.20 Adding comments helps you keep track of what is going on

What you have been playing with so far has been ActionScript set in **Normal** mode. If, however, you are happy with getting your hands dirty in lines of computer code, maybe you'll be comfortable working in **Expert** mode. You access Expert mode by clicking on the little arrow to the right of the **?** icon in the top right of Figure 11.22. This is what separates the men from the boys. In Expert mode:

- no parameter fields appear; you have to hard code the expressions yourself;
- the Up and Down arrows are switched off;
- in the button panel, only the Add (+) button works; you have to manually delete anything you don't want.

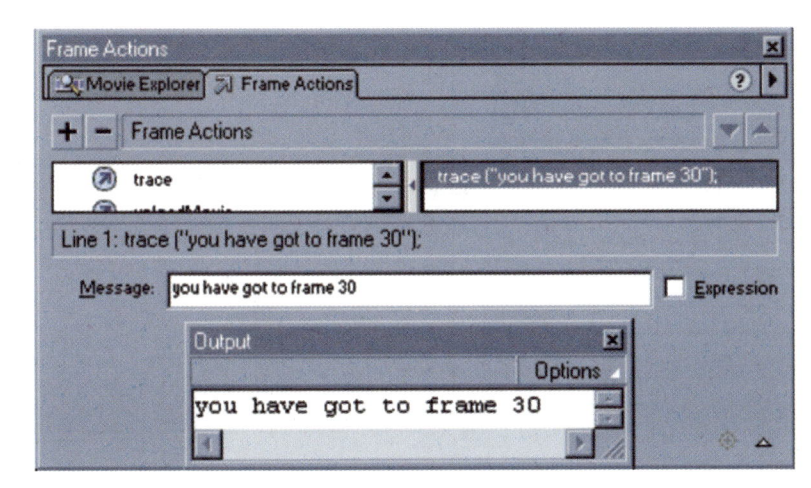

Figure 11.21 Using Trace to keep track of what is going on

So why would anyone want to switch to Expert mode? Well, it lets advanced users edit their scripts in an ordinary text editor just as they would JavaScript or VBScript. But unless you're proficient and confident in your programming abilities, you're best sticking with Normal mode!

Movie Explorer

Up till now you might have been wondering what that tab at the top of the Frame Actions dialog box labelled **Movie Explorer** is all about. Simply, it gives an overview of how your movie is constructed. And when you have a com-

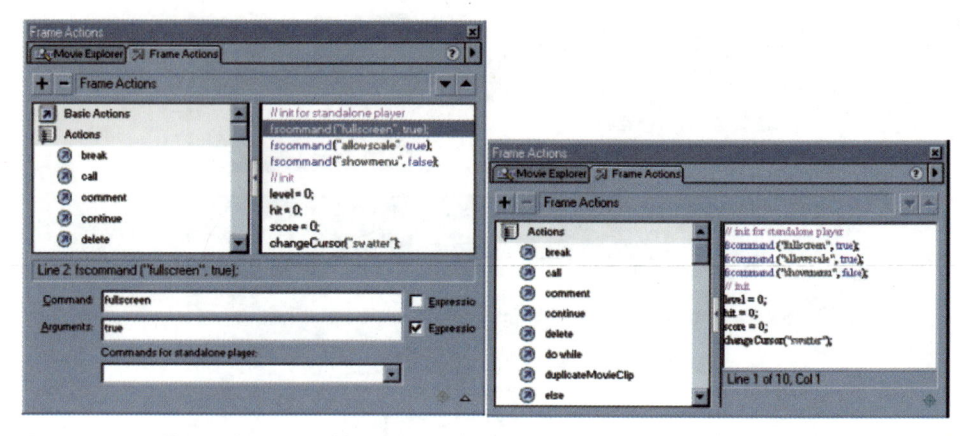

Figure 11.22 Frame Actions in Normal mode

plicated movie to deconstruct or to change, the Movie Explorer view will become a firm friend (Figure 11.23).

With the icon buttons along its top you can choose to show or hide:

- Text
- Buttons, Movie Clips and Graphics
- ActionScripts
- Video, sounds and bitmaps
- Frames and Layers.

And by choosing a suitable combination, you can find anything quickly and easily.

Coloured prompts

You might also have noticed something else in your experimentation with ActionScript, and that is the coloured prompts that Flash gives you to warn of trouble and to help you get your scripting accurate.

We've already noticed that if you make a scripting error, Flash highlights the relevant piece of code in red (Figure 11.8). But Flash also offers **syntax highlighting** to reassure you that your coding is correct:

- **Keywords** are blue;
- **Properties** are green;
- **Comments** are magenta;
- **Strings** in quotation marks are grey.

So if, for example, you typed in a keyword with incorrect capitalisation – say, loadmovienum instead of loadMovieNum – the word will no longer appear in blue.

As well as that, Macromedia is so anxious for you to up-skill that it encourages you not to use inelegant scripting solutions, even if they work. In Figure 11.24, for instance, you can see that *tellTarget* and *toggleHighQuality* are highlighted in green because Flash would rather you used **with** and **_highquality** instead.

To see examples of ActionScript with full explanations and extra tutorials, there are a number of web sites that offer just that. Point your browser at:

Interestingly enough, Flash deprecates tellTarget *in its Actions menu but not in its Basic Actions menu. Our advice is, if it works, don't worry unduly about it!*

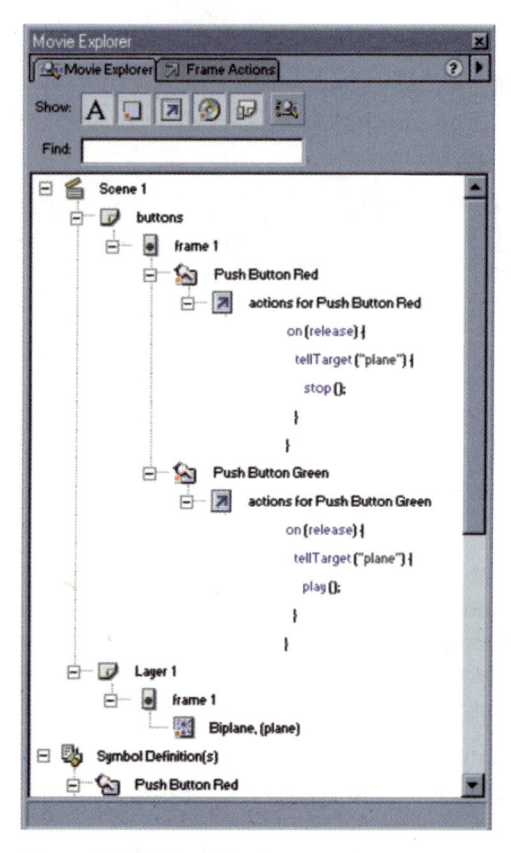

Figure 11.23 Movie Explorer mode

11: Complex interactivity

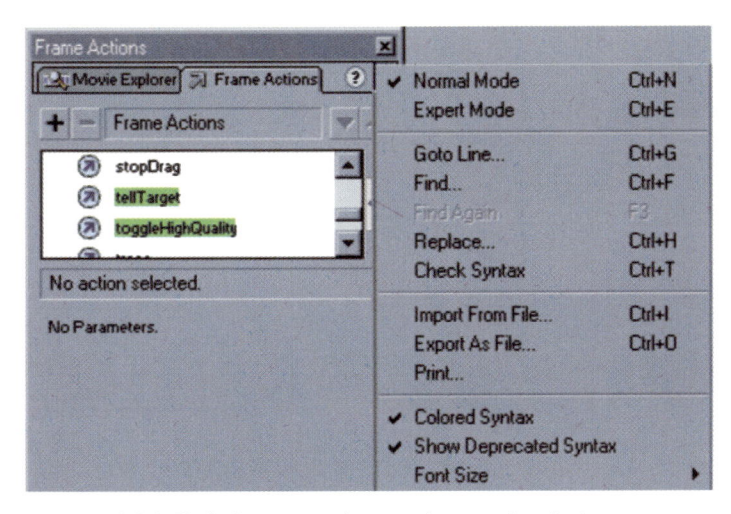

Figure 11.24 Flash deprecates the use of some of its Actions

- *http://www.flashkit.com*
- *http://www.flash4all.de*
- *http://www.flashheaven.de*
- *http://www.flashstudio.de*
- *http://www.flashzone.com*
- *http://www.actionscripts.org*
- *http://www.action-script.com*

Publishing your movies

12

Optimising your playback
Publishing your movies for use on the web
Publishing your movies as standalone Flash Player files
HTML publishing
Displaying alternative images
JPEG, PNG and QuickTime files
Projectors
Other image formats
Printing
Conclusion

Up till now we have been able to save our working files as Flash Movie – .fla – files, and it is important to understand the difference between these and the Player format – .swf – files. The former can be thought of as the development file standard. As we develop the movie, everything we create is saved in an all-encompassing Flash Movie file format, which we can return to in order to edit or change settings at any time.

The published Player format file can be set to prohibit editing by anyone else, stopping others from exploring its inner workings.

OK. We've created our Flash masterpiece and have tested it out using the *Test Movie* functions incorporated into our editor. The time has now come to publish our Flash movie to allow others to use it.

Flash files can be viewed in a number of ways, but the basis for everything is the Flash Player Format or .swf file. This format is the only one that supports all the functions that we have experimented with in creating our Flash project; however, you can export movies into 'lesser' formats such as bitmapped images, animated images, vector files and so on. They can also be viewed as standalone 'projector' files. We'll return to all of these shortly.

Optimising your playback

Perversely, before we start to export our movies, let's just pause for a moment to consider the all-important question of quality versus quantity. Naturally we want the final movie to be in as high a quality as possible. But, especially if the movie is to be viewed over the web, there is a price to pay for higher quality, and that is longer download times.

All web developers know that a happy compromise has to be struck between the quality and the size of image files and the time it takes to download that file. That compromise is all the more important in Flash since not only is the download time important because you don't want to keep your users waiting too long, but if you are using streaming video, the last thing you want is for the movie to stop and start as large chunks of animation try to squeeze down that narrow tube of available bandwidth.

There are many things that affect the overall file size of your final movie. For instance:

- a large number of bitmapped images;
- lots of keyframes;
- sounds;
- embedded fonts;
- gradients instead of plain fills;
- using individual graphic objects instead of symbols or groups.

However, Flash does not leave you to fend for yourself. It can simulate streaming of both video and audio and graphs your bandwidth so you can see at a glance which frames are likely to cause problems. The key to this help can be found when you test your movie (**Control:Test Movie**).

The debug menu of the Flash Player (*not* the editor) has some new options (Figure 12.1), which allow you to set the simulated download speed of a modem. You can see that the three most common modem speeds of 14.4, 28.8 and 56.6 kbps are listed, but you can also set them to whatever download speed you wish to simulate – allowing loading over a company intranet, via ISDN or even ADSL, for example.

Having set the simulated speed, you now need to go to your **View** menu and select **Bandwidth Profiler**. At the top of the screen Flash presents you with a graph which shows how much information is being transmitted along the Timeline of your movie (Figure 12.2), each bar representing the amount of data in each frame.

We've set our modem rate to 56.6 kbps for this example and you will see how a number of frames just nudge over the bottom line (which is coloured red). This

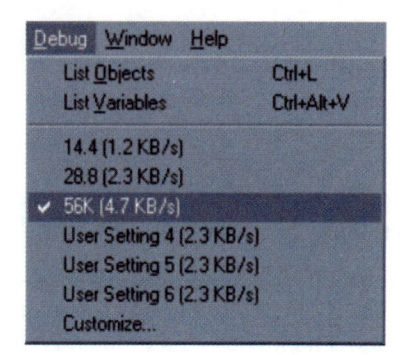

Figure 12.1 Setting your simulated download speed

warns us that at this particular modem speed these particular frames may cause the movie to pause a fraction while they download. (At a modem speed of 56.6 kbps, and with the frame rate set to 8 fps, the available bandwidth equates to around 4800 bytes per second, or 600 bytes per frame. If we had set the frame rate to the recommended 12 fps, then the available bandwidth would have been reduced to 4800/12 = 400 bytes per frame; and at this setting the amount of hesitation would be even greater.)

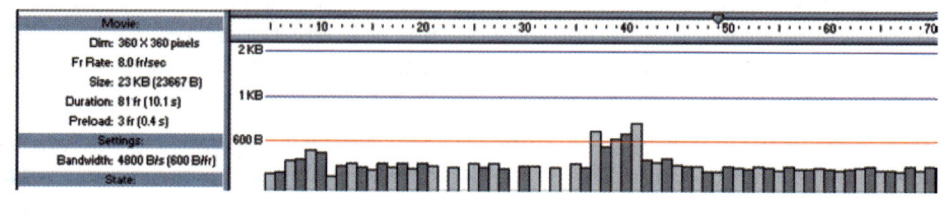

Figure 12.2 At this modem speed setting we may experience some pauses

Flash also shows how the movie will stream if we choose **View:Streaming Graph** from the player menu line. Each of the alternate bars of light and dark grey reflect the time taken to download that particular sector of information. When a frame contains very little information, you may well see more than one bar in a single time unit (as in Figure 12.3).

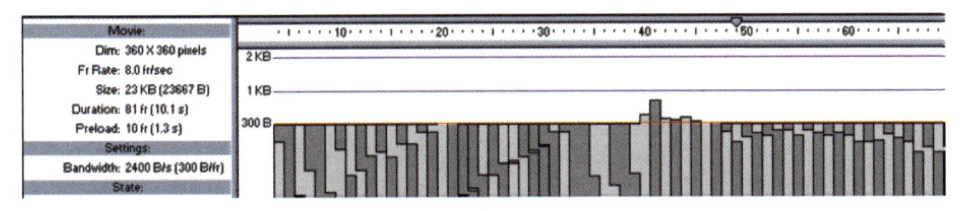

Figure 12.3 In streaming mode the width of the bar indicates how long it takes to download

*Flash can generate a printed report of the amount of information contained in your finished movie. When publishing the movie (see below) tick the box marked **Generate size report** under the Flash tab of the Publish Settings dialog box.*

Publishing your movies for use on the web

Flash's **Publish** command is used to create all the files necessary to view your Flash project file, even if the end user does not have a Flash player to view the finished file. As well as preparing a Flash Player (.swf) file, Publish can create alternative image formats (such as GIF, JPEG, PNG and QuickTime) for use on the web in the event that the Flash Player is not available and the user cannot (or will not) download the necessary player from the web. All the HTML code necessary to embed the finished file within a web document is created automatically and Publish can also generate standalone projectors for both the Windows and Macintosh computer systems.

When deciding on the formats that you wish Flash to generate you need to access the **Publish Settings** dialog box from the **File** menu (Figure 12.4). This allows you to publish in up to eight different formats as well as create the necessary HTML code for displaying the finished files in a browser.

*By default, Flash names your published files by adding the appropriate extension to the current file name. If you want to give them another name you should first deselect the **Use default names** checkbox shown in Figure 12.4.*

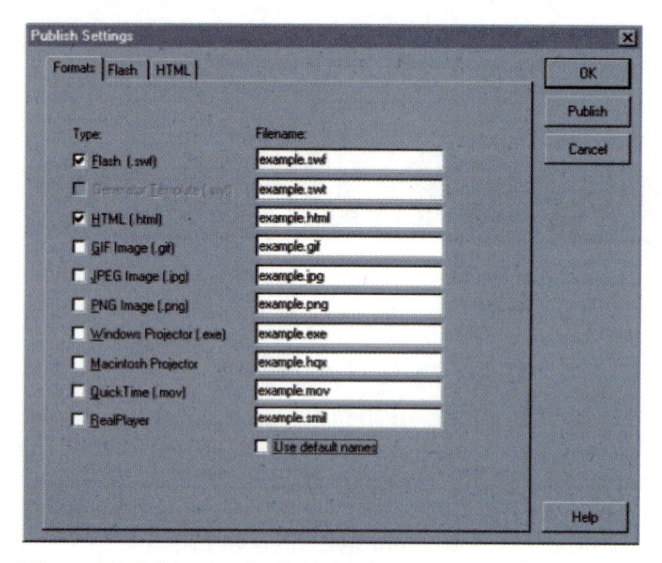

Figure 12.4 Selecting the Publish settings

Having chosen your preferred formats, you can instruct Flash to publish your movie by clicking on the **Publish** button on the top right corner of the dialog box, or by going to the **File** menu at a later time and selecting **Publish**. The published files are all stored in the same directory location as the original movie.

Publishing your movies as standalone Flash Player files

As well as allowing you to publish your movies for use on the web, or in a browser, Flash can also create standalone player applications.

First you need to select your publish options as described above and make sure that the **Flash (.swf)** check box (as shown in Figure 12.4) is ticked.

The middle tab in the Publish Settings dialog box is labelled **Flash**. Open this dialog box and you should see a list of options as shown in Figure 12.5.

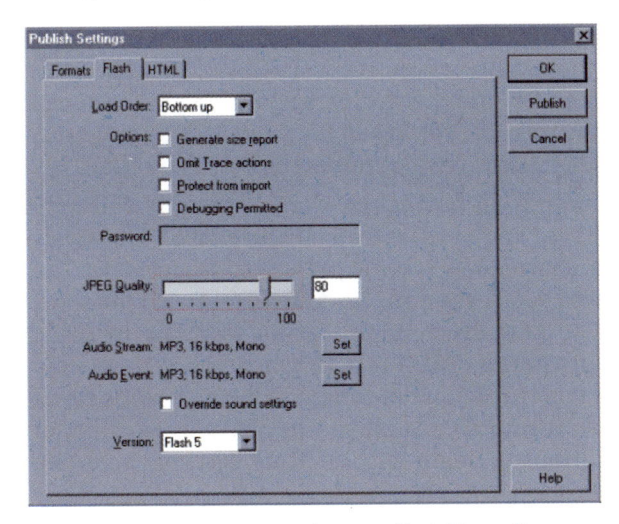

Figure 12.5 Setting options for your Flash Player file

- **Load Order:** this affects the download of the first frame. When a slow network or modem is being used, Flash draws individual layers in the order set by this option. With the choice set to *Bottom Up*, Flash begins to draw the lowest levels first.
- **Generate size report:** this option generates a printed report about the size of your movie.
- **Omit trace actions:** Trace comments add to the final size of your published movie file. Click here to remove them.
- **Protect from import:** by ticking here you can prevent others from importing your movie back into a Flash editor without first entering a password (set in the box beneath the checkboxes).
- **JPEG Quality:** The JPEG format is what is known as a lossy compression file. The more you compress your JPEG image, the worse its quality becomes. By moving the JPEG Quality slider (or by entering a specific value) you can determine the amount of compression you want for your JPEG images. A high figure gives the best quality; a low one optimises the download time.
- **Audio Stream and Event:** Use these buttons to override the rate and compression levels both for streaming and event sounds (Figure 12.6). Obviously for these settings to work there have to be sounds present in your movie! The compression pop-up menu gives you three choices: **ADPCM** is used for short event sounds. You can choose how much compression to apply to these sounds: 5-bit is the best quality option. **MP3** is used when you have mainly longer streaming sounds and you can again determine its quality settings. At settings lower than 20 kbps all sounds are played in mono, regardless of whether there was stereo content to begin with. A **Raw** setting causes no sound compression to be applied.

- **Override sound settings:** the above settings will defer to your original choice of sound compression unless this checkbox is ticked. This could be useful if you wanted to create two versions of your movie: one lower quality one for web use and another higher quality standalone version.
- **Version:** to maintain backwards compatibility you can publish your work as older Flash version movies. However, many of the functions may not work, especially if you set the value to anything lower than a Flash 4 movie format. Unless there is a very good reason not to do so, you should always select the Flash 5 option.

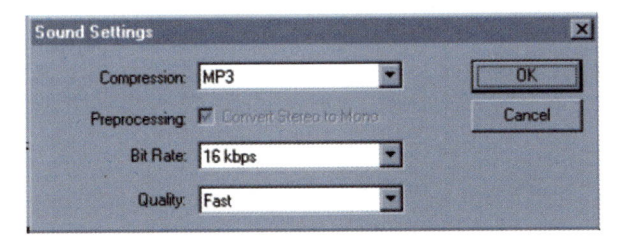

Figure 12.6 The Sound Settings dialog box

HTML publishing

In order to play a Flash movie in a web browser it is necessary to create the code to embed the .swf file into the HTML document.

By filling in blanks in a template depending on your choice of options, Flash can do a whole load of clever things such as detecting whether the browser used is capable of playing Flash movies and automatically downloading a player from the web if necessary.

The HTML options are set using the **Publish Settings** choice in your **File** menu and selecting the tab marked **HTML** (Figure 12.7).

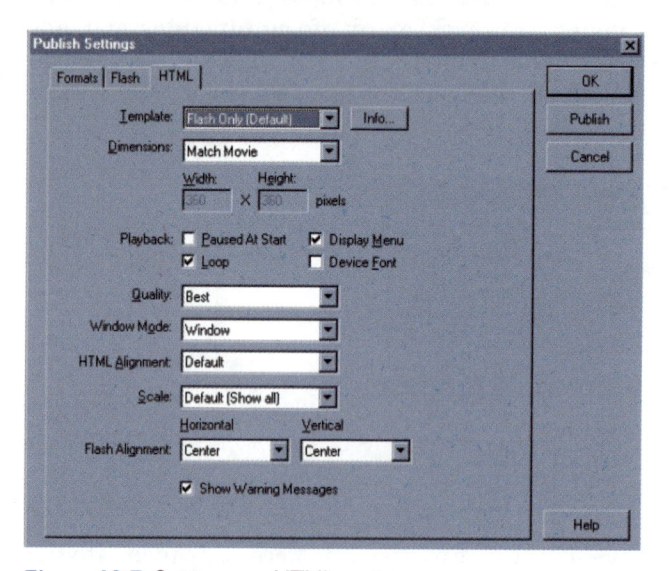

Figure 12.7 Setting your HTML options

- **Template:** from the drop-down menu you can choose one of a number of templates to use in creating your HTML file. The simplest is the one called *Flash Only (Default)*. This only allows users who have browsers equipped with the Flash Player to see your movie. Other viewers will be unable to see it. Some of the other template choices, however, create HTML code that displays alternative images if the Flash Player is not present. To find out what each template offers, click on the **Info** button to the right of the menu after you have made a selection.

- **Dimensions:** this option is used to determine the size of your final movie when played in the browser. The default is **Match Movie**, which sets the dimensions to those of the movie itself, but you can also choose to size the movie as an exact number of pixels wide and high, or as a percentage of the browser window.

- **Playback:** you are offered four choices to determine how the user views the final movie: **Paused at Start** requires the user to begin the movie manually – most probably by clicking a button or by choosing *Play* from the shortcut menu. **Loop** causes the movie to repeat when it reaches the last frame. **Display Menu** makes a shortcut menu available to users who right-click on the movie. If switched off, right-clicking will give information only about the Flash Player. **Device Font** substitutes anti-aliased system fonts for fonts that are not installed on the user's computer. This can speed up playback, but it works only on Windows systems; so if your movie is to be played on other platforms such as a Mac or Unix, you should leave this unselected.

- **Quality:** this setting allows you to balance quality against the speed of playback. **Low** switches anti-aliasing off permanently. **Autolow** allows Flash to switch on anti-aliasing if it finds that your computer can handle the downloading of individual frames. **Autohigh** assumes that anti-aliasing should be turned on unless the user's computer is unable to keep up with frame downloads. **High** gives priority to appearance over playback speed. With no animation, bitmaps are smoothed; otherwise they are not. **Best** smoothes all bitmaps and anti-aliasing is always switched on.

- **Window Mode:** for Windows users you can allow your movie's transparency options to permit other elements to move behind the movie using Dynamic HTML and either be hidden by the movie (**Opaque** setting) or show through (**Transparent Windowless**). This option is not available for users of other operating systems and Windows users must be using Internet Explorer v4 or above with the Flash Active X control.
- **HTML Alignment:** you can specify whether you want your movie aligned within the browser window in the Centre, Left, Right, Top or Bottom. **Scale**. If you specify width and height settings which are different from the movie's original size, you can determine whether Flash resizes the movie keeping the aspect ratio of the original, or whether it stretches either or both sides of the movie to be an exact fit within the browser frame.
- **Flash Alignment:** these settings determine how the movie is placed within its own window.
- **Show Warning Messages:** Flash can display a warning if there are any conflicts in the tag settings.

Displaying alternative images

Quite often on the web there will be people browsing who don't want to go to the bother of downloading a plug-in if their browser does not already support that standard. In such cases Flash can substitute animated or still images so that your viewer is not forced to look at a blank screen, or part of screen.

GIF images

If you have simple web animations, you could, for instance, substitute animated GIF files, which might take longer to download than the original Flash file but would at least offer something to see. In your Publish Settings dialog box, check the tick box marked GIF Image (Figure 12.4). A new tab appears at the top of the box marked GIF, which you should now open (Figure 12.8).

Once again, there are a number of options you can choose for your GIF file.

Choosing the GIF option will also automatically generate the necessary code in the resulting HTML file for substituting a GIF image if the Flash file cannot be played. The same is true of JPEG and PNG files.

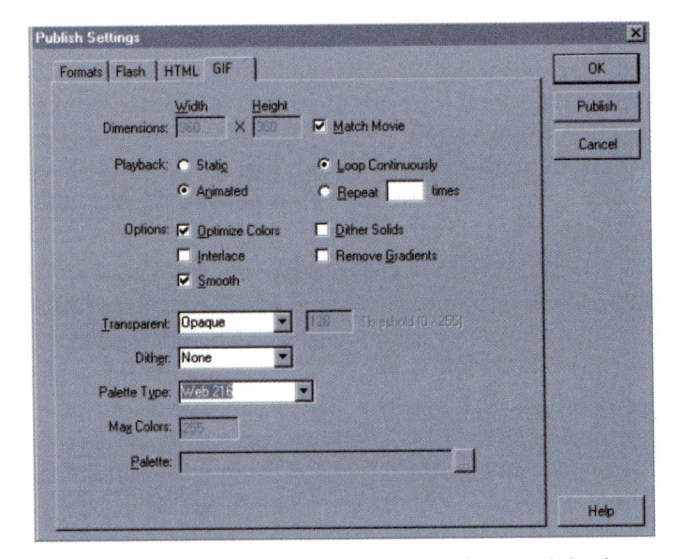

Figure 12.8 The GIF settings in the Publish Settings dialog box

- **Dimensions:** you can choose to have the GIF file the same size as the movie, or to determine the width and height of the image.
- **Playback:** you can choose whether you want a single static image to be substituted, or the entire animation exported as an animated GIF. If the latter, you can then determine how many times it should loop through its playback.
- **Options:** here you can specify a number of options affecting the appearance of the GIF: **Optimize colors** removes unused colours from the colour table, and thereby reduces the file size. **Smooth** enables or disables anti-aliasing. **Interlace** allows the exported GIF file to display incrementally rather than making the user wait for the entire image to download before being able to view it. **Dither Solids** applies dithering to solids as well as gradients, giving a seemingly larger palette than the web-safe palette would otherwise allow. **Remove Gradients** converts all gradient fills to solid fills, reducing file size and improving the colour since GIF gradients are often poor in quality due to the low number of available colours.
- **Transparent:** determines whether the background appears transparent or opaque, or whether colours below an alpha threshold appear transparent. This threshold can be given any number between 0 and 255. It is often a good idea to experiment with this setting.
- **Dither:** here you can specify which type of dithering, if any, you wish Flash to perform in order to approximate to all the colours with only a limited colour palette. **Ordered** provides the best dithering for the least possible file size increase. **Diffusion** creates the best dithering irrespective of file size.
- **Palette Type:** you can specify whether to use the Web 216 safe standard colour palette or customise the palette to your own specifications. The latter option often results in larger file sizes.

- **Max Colors:** if you select **Adaptive** or **Web Snap** options as your palette type, you can determine the maximum number of colours to be used in your GIF file.

JPEG, PNG and QuickTime files

Just as the GIF tab gives you a selection of options, so too do the JPEG and PNG tabs in the Publish Settings dialog box. The options are very similar, and therefore it should not be necessary for us to go through each of the settings again.

Suffice it to say, however, that whereas GIF files are ideal for line art drawings where there are large amounts of block colour, JPEGs are better for photographs and images that include gradients. In addition, the former are normally limited to 216 colours whereas JPEG files use the whole 16 million-colour palette.

PNG files can also support transparency (alpha channels) but despite their superior characteristics, their use is still limited on the world wide web.

QuickTime movies can be recognised both by Windows and Macintosh systems. Flash 5 creates QuickTime 4 format movies and these can recognise Flash's interactive features.

Projectors

For those who will view your movies without using a browser, Flash can create self-contained movie files, which play without the aid of external programs. Projector files are self-sufficient in that they contain everything needed to replay a Flash movie.

To create a projector file for Windows or Mac simply tick the checkbox(es) in the Publish Settings dialog box. There are no options to select for projector

You can create projector files for both Windows and Macintosh operating systems, but for the latter, Macintosh users need to convert the files using a program such as BinHex or Stuffit.

files, but Flash creates an .exe file for Windows users or an .hqx file for Mac users (Figure 12.9).

Figure 12.9 Windows and Mac projector files together with the original '.fla' file and the Shockwave (.swf) file

Other image formats

As well as exporting Flash movies as JPEG, GIF and PNG images, you can export individual frames as:

- EPS (Encapsulated PostScript)
- AI (Illustrator)
- PICT (Mac PICT)
- BMP (Windows Bitmap)
- WMF (Windows Metafile)
- EMF (Enhanced Metafile)
- DXF (Autocad DXF)
- SPL (FutureSplash Player)
- SWT (Generator Template).

You can achieve any of these exports by going to the **File** menu and selecting **Export Image**. Alternatively, to export the movie as a sequence of frames, go to **File:Export Movie**. In addition to the above formats you can export to:

- AVI (Windows Audio Visual)
- WAV (WAV audio)
- MOV (QuickTime Movie).

Printing

When developing your movie, Flash allows you to print out individual frames – or a number of frames together, somewhat as a storyboard layout – from the .fla file. From the **File** menu of the editor, choose **Page Setup** to determine page size, margins and whether you want the printer to print in portrait or landscape mode (Figure 12.10).

In the layout boxes you can choose whether you want to print out just the first frame or a selection of frames. If the latter, you should select **All frames** and then choose which pages you wish to print in the **Print** dialog box (Figure 12.11).

The last drop-down menu (**Layout**) allows you to specify whether you print out individual frames as single pages or as storyboard layouts (Figure 12.12).

Printing from a Flash movie

With version 5 of Flash came the introduction of one particular standard facility that many thought was long overdue in previous versions: that of being able to print particular pages from the movie that could be specified by the movie's author. But in addition, the new facility allows you to:

*You can choose to print each frame number underneath their individual thumbnail images by selecting the **Label frames** checkbox in Page Setup when you choose one of the Storyboard options.*

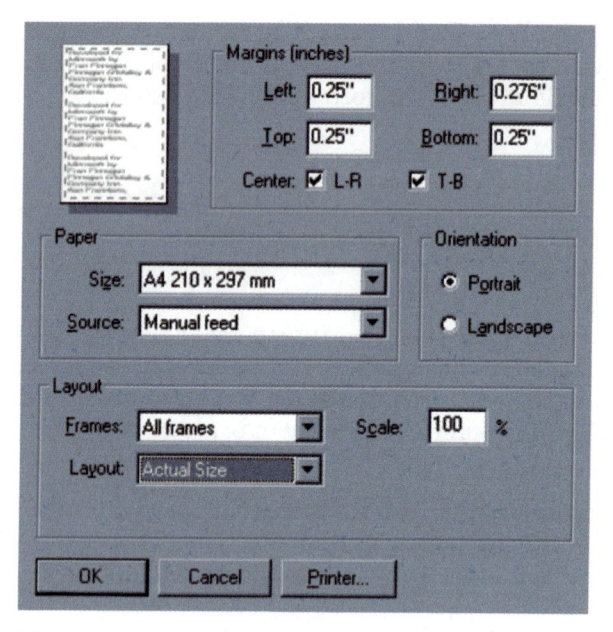

Figure 12.10 The Page Setup menu

- protect material in your movie from unauthorised printing;
- determine the print area of frames;
- specify if the printout should be as a vector image (giving higher resolution printing) or as a bitmapped image (to allow transparency and other effects);
- allow something to be printed out without it even being visible on screen!

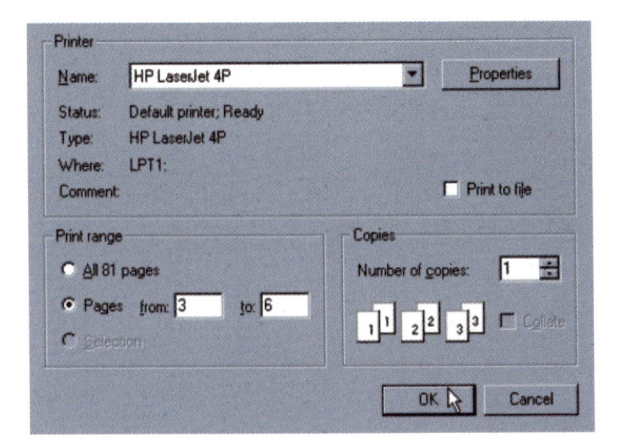

Figure 12.11 Determine which pages you want to print out from your Print dialog box

You specify which frames can be printed by opening up your **Frame Panel** and entering **#p** as the label for that particular frame (Figure 12.13).

It may well be that you don't want the entire movie area to print out, but just a small section of the screen. No problem! Create a frame that will not be viewed as part of the movie (perhaps at the very end of the Timeline) and create a shape, the size of the area you want printed. This time you should enter **#b** in the Frame Panel. You can do this only once per Timeline, and your bounding box will affect all printable frames in that Timeline.

To publish a movie with specific frames labelled for printing, the movie must be viewed with Flash Player version 4.0.25 or later. You can use a JavaScript routine to check for your users' player version, which Macromedia provides as part of its Deployment Kit. You can download this directly from the web at http://www.macromedia.com/software/flash/download/.

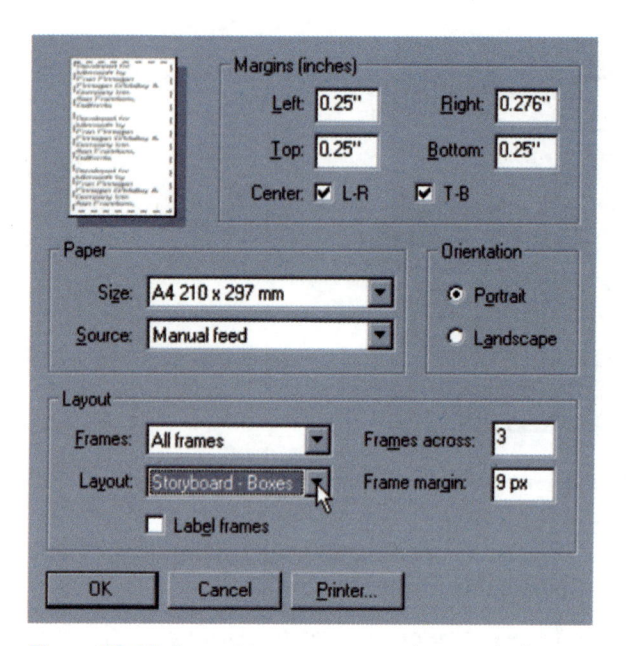

Figure 12.12 From this menu you can choose whether you want to print as individual pages or in a storyboard layout

If you specifically don't want *any* frames to be printed out by your end users, insert **!#p** in any frame's panel box. This also has the effect of dimming the *print* command from the right-click context menu.

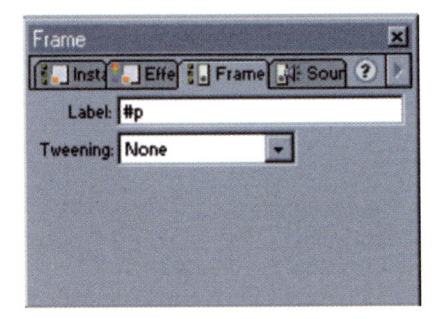

Figure 12.13 You specify printable frames in the Frame Panel

*You can, if you like, assign the **#p** label to a frame as part of a button instruction so that the movie frames print when you click on the button.*

Conclusion

Now that you have reached the end of this book you are only at the beginning of discovering the many and varied things you can do with Flash 5. Some of the tasks may look daunting at first, but experimentation really does make for familiarity, and we cannot over-emphasise how versatile and essential this package is for anyone wishing to create first-rate dynamic web sites and interactive movies.

For inspiration, you might like to visit two web sites that both use Flash extensively. One of our own web sites – *www.topspin-group.com* – uses Flash for its whole menu and navigation system, while *www.e-biz-pro.org* (the Association of eBusiness Professionals) is made up entirely using Flash.

Good luck in your creativity. The (animated) ball is now in your court!

Index

A

abstract variables, 185
actions, 150
    multiple-choice, 166–7
    order of carrying out, 153–4
    parameters for, 158
ActionScript, 184–213
    Expert mode, 208–9
    prompts, 211
    web sites, 211–13
ADPCM compression, 222
AI format, 230
alignment of objects, 53–4
alpha settings, 109–12, 132
alternative images, display of, 226–9
    formats for, 230–1
animated masks, 144–5
animated symbols, 145–7
anti-aliasing, 59, 225–6
Arrow tool, 39–41
Association of eBusiness Professionals, 235
AVI files, 231

B

bitmap graphics, 9, 216, 232
    conversion into vector files, 68–71
    import of, 64–7
    painting with, 71–6
Blend type menu, 138
BMP format, 230
Break Apart
    applied to bitmapped images, 72–3
    applied to instances, 114
    applied to text, 61
Brush tool, 32–4
buttons, 153, 160–4
    and interactivity, 164–5
    invisible, 167
    sounds added to, 174–5

C

Character panel, 57–8
circles, drawing of, 21–2
Clipboard (used for importing images), 67–8
colour
    of background, 14
    changes made by tweening, 131
    definition of, 24
    of instances, 108–12
    of keywords, properties, comments and strings (in *ActionScript*), 211
    null, 23
    selection of, 20, 23, 30
colour gradient, 21, 23
colour threshold, 69–71
comments
    on complex animations, 206, 208
    on frames 154–6
compression
    of images, 222
    of sound, 222–3
concrete variables, 185
conditional actions, 201–3
conversion
    of bitmapped images into vector files, 68–71
    of text into objects, 61
Copy command, 45
Copy Frames, 121

CorelDraw software, 64
corners
   creation of, 47
   shaping of, 24–6
creation of shapes and objects, 20–36
Cut command, 45

D

Debug menu, 217
Delete command, 45
deselection of objects, 42–3
device fonts, 58–9
dimensions of movies, 13
dithering, 228
download speeds, 216–19
dropper tool, 72–4
Duplicate command, 45–6
dustbin, 81, 84
DXF format, 230
dynamic text, 188

E

editing
   commands for, 45
   of multiple frames, 125–6
   of sound files, 180–2
   of symbols, 113
ellipses, drawing of, 21
e-mail, 195
embedded fonts, 58–9
EMF format, 230

EPS format, 64, 230
Eraser tool, 34–5
error highlighting (in *ActionScript*), 211, 213
event sounds, 170, 177
expressions, mathematical, 185

F

fading in and out
   of images, 131–2
   of sound, 180–1
Faucet tool, 34
files
   formats of, 64–5, 216, 219–20
   loading of, 192
   size of, 216–17
fills, 20, 30–1
Fireworks software, 67
FLA format, 216
flipping
   of objects, 51–2
   of text, 60
FLW500 number, 8
fonts, 57–9
   export of, 59
formats *see* files
frame actions, 150–4
frame-by-frame animation, 122–8
   for creating moving masks, 144–5
frame rate, 13, 125–7

frames, 116
   comments added to, 154–6
   labelling of, 154–6, 233–4
   numbering of, 231
   previewing of, 127
   printing of, 231–3
   reversal of, 143–4
   sequential playback of, 123
   sound added to, 173
   see also keyframes
Freehand software, 64
FS Command, 205–7

G

Gap Size icon, 31–2
Generator 2 application, 2
Get URL action, 192–5
GIF images, 227
Go To action, 158
gradient, 21, 23
gradient fill, 30–1
graphics
   import of, 64–8
   symbols created from, 105, 107
grids, 15, 17
grouping of objects, 54
guide layers
   creation of, 91
   and guided layers, 86–7
   for moving objects, 135

Index

H
hardware requirements for *Flash 5*, 2
hidden elements *see* mask layers and masked layers
Hit state, 160, 163–4, 167
hot spots, 164
HTML publishing, 223–6

I
'If' statement, 204
'If ... Else' statement, 204
'If frame is loaded' statement, 201–3
Illustrator software, 64, 67, 230
image formats generated by *Flash 5*, 219
import
    of images, 64–8
    of sounds, 170–3
Ink Bottle tool, 35–6
Ink Mode, 28
installation of *Flash* software, 2–7
instances, 98, 105, 107
    making changes to, 108–12
    colour of, 131
    resizing of, 133
    swapping of, 112–13
    unlinked from their symbols, 114
interactivity
    formulaic, 184
    using buttons, 164–5
Internet Explorer, 226

J
JPEG images, 222, 227, 229

K
kerning, 58–9
keyframes, 66, 117–21
    clearance and deletion of, 122
    insertion of, 121, 130
    virtual, 122

L
Lasso tool, 41–2
layers, 12, 80
    creation and deletion of, 81–4, 94
    locking of, 84
    naming of, 81–2
    stacking of, 83
    types of, 86–7
    viewed as outlines, 84–5, 88
    visibility of, 84
libraries of symbols, 98
    use counts, 103–5
Library directory, 101
Line tool, 20–1
lines
    repositioning of, 46
    smoothing of, 26–7
    width of, 20
Load Movie action, 192, 195–6
looping
    of animations, 203
    of frames, 123
    of sounds, 178
lossy compression files, 222

M
Magic Wand tool, 76–7
mask layers and masked layers, 87, 91–4
    animation of, 144–5
    sound added to, 172–3
modification of objects, scope for, 38
morphing, 128, 137–42
motion guides and motion paths, 86, 134–6
    used with shape tweens, 143
motion tweening, 128–36
    colour changes by means of, 131
    combined with shape tweening, 154
    for creating moving masks, 144–5
MouseEvent actions, 164–5
MOV format, 231
movie clips, 145–7, 195–7
    unique identification of, 197
Movie Explorer, 209–10, 212
Movie Properties, 13–14
MP3 files, 170, 222

N
Netscape Navigator, xi

O
Object Inspector, 44
onion skinning, 123–5, 139

Index

orientation to motion paths, 136
outlines, layers viewed as, 84–5, 88
Oval tool, 21–2

P

Paint Bucket, 29–30
Paint Shop Pro software, 64, 68
painting
    with bitmapped images, 71–6
    options for, 32–4
panels, 15
Paragraph panel, 59
Paste command, 45–6
Paste Frames, 121
Paste in place, 95
Paste Special, 46, 68
Pen tool, 27
Pencil tool, 26–7
PICT format, 230
Play action, 157
playback, 2
    of frames, 123
    optimization of, 216
    options for, 18
    plug-in for, 5
Player format files, 216
PNG files, 227, 229
point size, 59–60
Polygon mode, 42–3
printing
    from movies, 231–5
    prevention of, 234
projector files, self-sufficient, 229–30
protection
    of frames from printing, 234
    of movies from re-importing, 222
publication of movies, 219–21
    in HTML, 223–6
    as standalone files, 221–3

Q

Quick Time 4 format, 65, 170, 229

R

raster graphics *see* bitmap graphics
Rectangle tool, 24–5
repositioning
    of line segments, 46
    of objects, 43–4
reshaping of filled areas, 48
resizing
    of instances, 133
    of objects, 48–51
reversal of frames, 143–4
rotation
    of instances, 108
    of objects, 51–2, 134
    of text, 60
rulers and ruler units, 12–13 15, 17

S

saving of animations, 145–6
Scale command, 48–50
scaling
    of instances, 108
    of text blocks, 60
scenes, 147–8
'scrubbing', 178–9
selection of objects, 38–9
    partial, 42
    using Arrow tool, 39–41
    using Lasso tool, 41–2
    see also deselection of objects
Setup, types of, 5–7
Setup.exe file, 2
shape hints, 141–2
shape tweening, 137–43
    combined with motion tweening, 154
    for creating moving masks, 144–5
    with multiple objects, 139–40
size reports, 219, 222
skewing
    of objects, 51–2
    of text, 60
smoothing
    of animation, 123, 128
    of curves, 27–8
    of lines, 26–7
snapping
    to grids, 15, 17
    to objects, 91
sounds
    added to buttons, 174–5

Index

added to frames, 173
compression of, 222–3
editing of, 180–2
import of, 170–3
looping of, 178
preview of, 171–2
simultaneous playing of, 176
starting of, 177–8
SPL format, 230
stacking
   of actions, 166–7
   of layers and objects, 83, 89–90
Stage area, 10–12
   options for control of, 12–13
   size of, 13–14
Start Menu, 8
Start sound instruction, 177–8
static text, 188–9
Stop command, 157
   for sound, 176–7
storyboard layouts, 231, 234
streaming, 9–10
   simulation of, 202, 217–19
   of sounds, 170, 178–9
strokes, 20
Sun AU files, 170
.swf files, 64, 216
SWT format, 230
symbols

created from graphic objects, 105, 107
created without conversion, 106–7
deletion of, 103, 105
editing of, 113
folders of, 102–3
libraries of, 98
special collections of, 102
use of, 108
Sync settings, 175–8
syntax highlighting (in *ActionScript*), 211, 213
system requirements for *Flash 5*, 2

T

teaser animations, 202–3
Tell Target action, 195–201
testing
   of actions, 206
   of buttons, 163
   of movies and scenes, 18, 159
text
   blocks treated as objects, 61
   insertion of, 56–8
   paragraph attributes, 59
   scaling, rotation, skewing and flipping of, 60
   static and dynamic, 188–9
Timeline, xi, 10–12
   repositioning of, 11

used to control layers, 86–8
viewing of, 11, 120
tinting of objects, 131
Toolbox, 10, 15
tooltips, 15, 17, 156
trace actions, 206, 209, 222
Transform Inspector, 49–50
transformation of text blocks, 60
transparency of instances, 108–12
tweening *see* frame-by-frame animation; motion tweening; shape tweening

U

uniform resource locators (URLs), 192–5
use counts, 103–5

V

vector graphics, 9, 216, 232
   converted from bitmapped images, 68–71
   import of, 64, 66–7
versions of *Flash*, 223
visibility order, 54

W

WAV files, 170–1, 231
web sites, 211–13, 235
While command, 204–5
WMF format, 230